Books by Bill Myers

NON-FICTION

Hot Topics, Tough Questions
Christ B.C.

FICTION

JOURNEYS TO FAYRAH
The Portal
The Experiment
The Whirlwind
The Tablet

Blood of Heaven (Adult Fiction)

FORBIDDEN DOORS (Teen Series)

THE INCREDIBLE WORLDS OF WALLY MCDOODLE (Youth Series)

BOOK AND VIDEO SERIES

MCGEE AND ME!

9609

BILL MYERS

HOT TOPICS TOUGH QUESTIONS

BETHANY HOUSE PUBLISHERS
MINNEAPOLIS, MINNESOTA 55438

Published by Bethany House Publishers
A Ministry of Bethany Fellowship, Inc.
11300 Hampshire Avenue South
Minneapolis, Minnesota 55438

Printed in the United States of America.

Library of Congress Cataloging-in-Publication Data

Myers, Bill, 1953–
    Hot topics, tough questions : honest answers to your hardest questions / Bill Myers.
       p. cm.
    ISBN 1-55661-870-0
    1. Youth—Religious life—Juvenile literature. 2. Christian life—Juvenile literature. [1. Christian life. 2. Conduct of life.] I. Title.
BV4531.2.M94   1996
248.8'3—dc21
                                         96–45770
                                            CIP
                                            AC

For Nicole and Mackenzie—

As the Lord continues to make you ". . . mature
and complete, not lacking anything."

James 1:4

BILL MYERS is a youth worker and a creative writer and film director who co-created the "McGee and Me!" book and video series and whose work has received over forty national and international awards. A Christian with a deep faith and a commitment to encourage others toward spiritual growth, he has many books published and several films and videos in distribution, including the popular *Fast Forward* video series, a companion to this book. He and his family make their home in California.

CONTENTS

CHAPTER 1

How Do I Find God's Will?

owie was going to be a superjock. He had the bod, the brains, and the will. Every day he was at the local batting cage practicing his swing. Every day he'd work on catching flies, fielding grounders, running bases. Finally the first day of tryouts rolled around, and Howie was ready.

Of course, he was a bit surprised when the coach made him put on the helmet and shoulder pads. And a little confused when he was forced to line up facing seven other guys. But that was nothing compared to what he felt when someone in the middle yelled "hike" and a 208-pound mountain of flesh slammed into him, ran up his chest, tap-danced on his head for half an hour, and finally ran down his back to tackle the guy with the ball.

By the time Howie was released from the hospital, the season was practically over. But as I said, the guy was determined. He began practicing his tackling, his passing, his punting. And by the time the next tryout rolled around, Howie was ready.

Of course, he was a little surprised to learn they were holding it in the gym. And he was a little bugged that they made him exchange his pads and cleats for shorts and basketball shoes. But what really ticked Howie off was that the coach threw him out of the game for tackling the guy with the ball. I mean, wasn't that supposed to be the whole idea?

Needless to say, Howie had a little problem.

It had nothing to do with his strength, his ability, or even his dedication. The problem was that he just didn't know what game he was playing. He didn't know the rules.

An absurd story? Of course.

But how many people sign up for this program called "Christianity" without ever really bothering to check out the rules, learn the objectives, or find out what the Coach really wants?

What *does* God want? Why am I here? What's the purpose? How can I find God's will for my life?

Important questions. And in our survey among Christian teens, questions about finding God's will ranked number one.

So . . . let's see if we can come up with a few answers.

Why Are We Here?

First of all, we humans were created for one reason: to be friends with God—to have fellowship with Him, to give Him pleasure.

> Thou art worthy, O Lord, to receive glory and honor and power: for thou hast created all things, and for *thy pleasure they are and were created* (Revelation 4:11, KJV, italics added).

We used to give God that pleasure; we used to have that friendship—way back in the beginning, back in the Garden. But it wasn't too long before we told Him to take a hike, before we made it clear that we wanted to do things our way, not His.

And by doing so we pulled the plug on that special friendship.

And, being the gentleman He is, God stepped aside to let us have our way. It must be tough watching us slowly destroy ourselves with hatred, lust, fear, war.

And it must be unbearable hearing the very ones He created for fellowship use His name only when they're cussing someone out. But since that's what we seem to want, God is polite enough to let us have our way.

Still, for those of us who've realized that our way may not be the best, for those of us who want to return to that original friendship with God, He has provided a way—Jesus Christ. Jesus acts as a door, a passageway that leads us back into that friendship with God. All we have to do is be willing to walk through. Jesus does the rest. In fact, Jesus himself said,

> I am the door; if anyone enters through Me, he shall be saved (John 10:9, NASB).

> I am the way and the truth and the life. No one comes to the Father except through me (John 14:6).

These are just two of hundreds of verses that make it clear there's a way to come back to God. Anyone can do it. All you have to do is ask Jesus to take the punishment for your sins and agree to let Him be the boss of your life. It's that simple.

And for those of us who have made that decision, for those who want to spend life as friends with God (both now and for eternity), the Lord has a very special plan. It's called,

"Come here, sit on My throne, and rule the universe with Me."

What?

The Eternal Plan

That's right. You see, according to the Bible, God's eternal, long-range plan for His children, for those who've chosen to return to Him, is for us to help Him rule the universe. Find that a little hard to swallow? I did. But it's right there in the Book:

> To him who overcomes, I will give the right to
> sit with me on my throne, just as I overcame
> and sat down with my Father on his throne
> (Revelation 3:21).

Or how 'bout Romans 8:

> The Spirit himself testifies with our spirit that
> we are God's children. Now if we are children,
> then we are heirs—heirs of God and co-heirs
> with Christ, if indeed we share in his suffer-
> ings in order that we may also share in his
> glory (Romans 8:16–17).

There's more:

> Do not be afraid, little flock, for your Father
> has been pleased to give you the kingdom
> (Luke 12:32).

And finally:

> Do you not know that the saints [that's us]
> will judge the world? . . . Do you not know
> that we will judge angels? (1 Corinthians 6:2,
> 3).

That's God's ultimate plan for us. That's the object
of the game—to share in His glory and to co-rule His
universe.

Awesome? Yes.

Incredible? Yes.

Impossible? No.

Not with God. You see, that's the nice thing about
having His own universe. He can run it however He
wants. He can bless whomever He chooses. And for
some reason He has chosen us.

There's only one snag. We're not quite ready. We
need to go through a little renovation, a little repair, a
little scrubbing up. The centuries of sin have taken
their toll on our bodies, minds, and emotions. Each of

us is filled to the brim with fear, guilt, and sin. In short, the bad news is we're all in one sense or another spiritually sick.

But not for long. . . .

The Lifelong Plan

You see, being a Christian is a lot more than getting to heaven and cashing in on those mansions. God's love for us is so great that as soon as we say yes to Him, He sets His lifelong plan for us into action.

Which is. . . ?

> . . . that you may be mature and complete, not lacking anything (James 1:4).

God wants to heal us. He wants to clean out and mend all the wounds the world has gouged into us. He wants us free and whole. In short, God wants to make us as complete and fulfilled as we were when He originally made us.

That's it. That's all He wants. Despite the rumors, He's not some ogre with a whip, demanding that we follow a bunch of outdated rules and regulations. He's not some screaming boot camp sergeant barking out orders to make sure life is unbearable. On the contrary, Jesus said, "I came that they might have life, and might have it abundantly" (John 10:10, NASB).

That's what God wants. He wants us to experience this creation of His, this thing called "life" at its absolute maximum. He wants us to experience the greatest joy, the greatest peace, the greatest love. . . . He wants us to experience *totally* complete, *totally* full, *totally* ABUNDANT life.

That's why God hates sin so much. Not because He's against people having a good time. But because sin steals that life from us. It ties us up. It robs us of enjoying all that we could enjoy, of being all that we could

13

be. Sure, sin may look good on the outside; it may be pleasant to the eye and sweet to the taste. But inside it always has a hook . . . ALWAYS. And once we swallow that hook it starts to take control. Oh, it's barely noticeable at first, but gradually it starts to pull and control. And before we know it, sin gets its way—stealing and robbing us of that abundant life God wants us to have.

As we go through the questions in this book, keep in mind that God's answers are not intended to snuff out our good times. It's just the opposite. His answers are there to help us enjoy the pleasures of life more deeply. He's on *our* side. He always wants the best for us. And He loves us so much that He will discipline or even fight us if we try to settle for second rate, for something that will ultimately steal His very best from us.

OK, so God's eternal plan is for us to share His throne. And His lifelong plan is to make us whole and complete. Fine. But how does that help me decide what I should do for a living? Or what classes I should take next semester? Or whether I should go out with sexy Stan with the roving hands?

God's Immediate Will

Actually, knowing God's lifelong plan in your life really does help in the making of day-to-day decisions. If you know He wants you "mature and complete, not lacking anything" (James 1:4), chances are you'll try to follow that plan.

But if you're still not sure, there are six very easy ways to find God's immediate will in your life—six ways to help you make those day-to-day decisions. And if three or four seem to point in the same direction, chances are that's the direction you should be heading.

1. READ GOD'S WORD

This is easily the most important way of finding out God's will. There are several reasons for this importance, but the main one is the incredible power of His Word. Remember, it was with God's spoken Word that He actually created the universe.

And remember when Jesus and Satan were battling it out during Jesus' temptation? They didn't use guns, tanks, or bombs—they didn't even try to nuke each other. Instead, the Creator of the universe and the most evil force in the universe both knew the most powerful weapon in the universe. They fought with one thing and one thing only: God's Holy Word, the Bible (Matthew 4:1–11).

There's something terribly powerful, something supernatural about God's Word. First of all, it's "God-breathed" (2 Timothy 3:16). Somehow a part of God's very life is in those words. And since they have His life, as we read and study them, they begin to change us. . . .

- They cleanse (Ephesians 5:26).
- They encourage (Romans 15:4).
- They equip us to do good (2 Timothy 3:16–17).
- They even give faith (Romans 10:17).

Pretty powerful stuff.

As we dwell on God's Word, we actually find ourselves starting to think more like Him, to act more like Him, and *to make the decisions He would have us make*.

It's like hanging around a close friend. We don't go around consciously trying to imitate each other. But gradually, as we spend more and more time together, we start to think more and more alike. We start saying and doing some of the same things.

That's the sort of friendship and closeness God is looking for. Not because He's an egotist and wants a bunch of God-clones walking around. But because He knows that when we think and act like Him, we tend to be much happier.

Unfortunately none of this learning and understanding happens overnight. There are no pills for instant wisdom, no hot-line numbers for making godly decisions. God does not want mindless puppets. He wants friends. And as we spend time with Him in His Word, that friendship just *naturally* develops. We begin to naturally think and speak as He does. We begin to naturally develop "the mind of Christ." And, quite often, we begin to just naturally do what He would have us do.

So if you haven't started to read God's Word on a daily basis, do it. If you have, keep it up. It will give you clear guidelines and principles to help you in nearly every area of decision-making.

2. PRAY FOR WISDOM

Another way of finding out God's will is through prayer:

> If any of you lacks wisdom, he should ask God, who gives generously to all without finding fault, and it will be given to him (James 1:5).

That's quite a promise. And it's true. Despite what it feels like sometimes, God is not into playing hide-and-seek with His will. Chances are He wants you to know His will even more than you do. So ask.

It's doubtful you'll be receiving any "angel-grams" or instructions carved in stone (although both have been known to happen). But somehow, some way, if you're really serious, He'll let you know what you should do. It may not be in your timing or in your way—but rest assured, you will know. You have my word on it.

Better yet, you have His.

3. SEEK COUNSEL

As much as you may be convinced that nobody has gone through what you're going through, chances are you're wrong. Other people have passed your way—

maybe not the exact steps, but close enough. Take advantage of *their* experiences. Take advantage of *their* mistakes. That's one of the reasons God keeps us older Christians puttering around out there—so you can seek our counsel.

If you have a decision to make, talk to your pastor (that's what he's there for). Talk to your Sunday school teacher, or youth worker, or some older Christian you respect. In fact (and I know this may sound radical), try talking to your parents. Even they've been known to be right from time to time.

4. LISTEN TO THE HOLY SPIRIT

If you are a Christian, remember—you have a bit of God living inside you. Trust His guidance. Trust His nudgings. See if that "still, small voice" inside isn't encouraging you along a certain path. Sometimes this can be tricky because your "wants" may be so loud they drown out what the Holy Spirit is saying. But if you wait and continue to listen, there's a good chance you'll sense what you should do.

> But when he, the Spirit of truth, comes, he will guide you into all truth. He will not speak on his own; he will speak only what he hears, and he will tell you what is yet to come (John 16:13).

5. ASK, "DOES IT GLORIFY GOD?"

That's not a real popular question these days—especially with so many of us human types only looking out for ourselves. But if we were originally created to please God (Revelation 4:11), then we'll only be the happiest when we're doing just that.

Now, that doesn't mean we all have to become missionaries or start passing out tracts to every Tom, Dick, or Harriet. But it does mean "whatever you do, do it all for the glory of God" (1 Corinthians 10:31).

If it's cutting down trees or cutting out cookies, it's still possible to do it in a way that will glorify God. Maybe it's simply your attitude toward God as you're doing it. Maybe it's letting Him shine through you to your co-workers. Who knows? But if what you want to do doesn't glorify God, take a good hard look at it. It may not be what He has in mind.

The last way of determining God's will is . . .

6. LOOK AT THE CIRCUMSTANCES

This can be the trickiest of all. Sometimes God wants us to close our eyes against all the circumstances and just step out blindly in faith. Other times He wants us to look clearly at the facts and make a decision based on them. If I think circumstances are important in making a decision, I'll write a list of all the pros and cons. Then, *only after I've put all the other methods to work* (studying God's Word, praying, getting counsel, waiting on the Holy Spirit, and asking if it glorifies God), I'll make the decision.

These are six easy ways to find out God's will in day-to-day living. Again, you may not need to use all of them. If three or four seem to point in the same direction, that may be all the confirmation you need.

But whatever you decide, once you've waited on the Lord and made your decision, step out and do it. Don't be so frightened of making a mistake that you do nothing. If you're wrong, God's not going to clobber you over the head. He's on your side, remember?

He may correct, He may change your course, He may even do a little disciplining if necessary. But if you honestly seek His will, you'll always find it.

If you sincerely seek God's will in your life, it will be *impossible* for you to miss it. It's a promise. . . .

> I will instruct thee and teach thee in the way which thou shalt go: I will guide thee with mine eye (Psalm 32:8, KJV).

The steps of a good man are ordered by the LORD. (Psalm 37:23, KJV).

For this God is our God for ever and ever; he will be our guide even to the end (Psalm 48:14).

CHAPTER 2

What Is God Really Like?

To know what God is really like we don't have too much to go on besides what the Bible says. I mean, it's not like He does guest spots on *The Tonight Show* or you can whip out your billfold and look at His latest snapshot. But the Bible does a pretty good job of describing Him. In fact, if you were to list just the passages that explain what God is like, you'd wind up with a book over twice the size of this one.

So, what is He like? I mean, are we talking Wizard of Oz *time with the booming voice and puffs of smoke, or is He some white-bearded old duffer shuffling around, or what? Does He really have a personality? Or is He just some cosmic force that is everywhere and in everything?*

God has personality—a very definite personality. He has specific likes and dislikes—things that please Him and things that peeve Him. He has character traits that you'd expect to see only in an infinite Being, and others that you can find in the guy next door.

The Unique Qualities

God has some characteristics that are His and His alone. For instance, He's . . .

INFINITE

He was not created. He never had a beginning; He'll never have an end. Scripture is pretty clear about the matter:

> How great is God—beyond our understanding! The number of his years is past finding out (Job 36:26).

> Before the mountains were born or you brought forth the earth and the world, from everlasting to everlasting you are God (Psalm 90:2).

And while we're talking about infinite, how about size?

> Even the highest heaven cannot contain you (1 Kings 8:27).

> "Do not I fill heaven and earth?" declares the LORD (Jeremiah 23:24).

THE CREATOR

The fact that God created all things probably doesn't come as too great a shock to you. But for some it's a bit of a surprise to learn that it was God the Son who did the creating. In a few pages we'll cover more on how Jesus fits into the God picture, but for now take a look at what Scripture says about His creative abilities:

> For by him [Jesus] all things were created: things in heaven and on earth, visible and invisible, whether thrones or powers or rulers or authorities; all things were created by him and for him (Colossians 1:16).

> In these last days he has spoken to us by his Son, whom he appointed heir of all things, and through whom he made the universe (Hebrews 1:2).

THE SUPREME BOSS

God is the One in charge; no one even runs a close second.

Yours, O LORD, is the greatness and the power and the glory and the majesty and the splendor, for everything in heaven and earth is yours. Yours, O LORD, is the kingdom; you are exalted as head over all. Wealth and honor come from you; you are the ruler of all things. In your hands are strength and power to exalt and give strength to all (1 Chronicles 29:11–12).

ALL-KNOWING

The eyes of the LORD are everywhere (Proverbs 15:3).

Nothing in all creation is hidden from God's sight. Everything is uncovered and laid bare before the eyes of him to whom we must give account (Hebrews 4:13).

ALL-POWERFUL

With God all things are possible (Matthew 19:26).

For nothing is impossible with God (Luke 1:37).

UNCHANGING

This has an up side and a down side. The good news is that in this frantic, ever-changing world of ours—where what's in this morning is out this evening, where promises are made to be broken, where relationships are as disposable as Kleenex—it's great to know God will always stay unshakable in His integrity, honesty, and faithfulness.

I the LORD do not change (Malachi 3:6).

God is not a man, that he should lie, nor a son of man, that he should change his mind (Numbers 23:19).

But this also means that God's principles and standards won't be dictated by the latest trends and whims; even at the risk of being "uncool," God will stay the same. He would rather be uncool than be unfaithful.

Unfortunately that often makes His standards (and followers) seem outdated. But it's a small price to pay since, as we've already discussed, His methods wind up being the best anyway.

HOLY

God is so pure and intensely good that no one can even stand in His presence. In fact, when He came down to talk with Moses on top of Mount Sinai, He warned the people not even to touch the mountain or they'd die (Exodus 19:12).

Whew!

Another time over 50,000 men were struck dead by looking into the ark of the covenant (where God's presence dwelt). The remaining survivors probably put it best when they said,

> Who can stand in the presence of the LORD,
> this holy God? (1 Samuel 6:20).

It's as if God is this incredibly pure goodness, this intense perfection that vaporizes any imperfection that comes close to Him. That's why the cleansing power of Jesus' blood is so important. Without Jesus to take all of our imperfections upon himself, we could never approach God—much less live to tell about it.

What Does God Look Like?

A good question. Because of God's holiness it's pretty hard to tell. In fact, it's because of this holiness that those who have gotten close to Him can describe only this incredibly intense light.

God, the blessed and only Ruler, the King of kings and Lord of lords, who alone is immortal and who lives in unapproachable light, whom no one has seen or can see (1 Timothy 6:15–16).

Oh, there is one person who has seen God—sort of. It happened to Moses, and it's one of my favorite accounts in the Old Testament.

As Moses and God were becoming better and better friends, Moses began asking if it was possible to see Him. He wasn't asking out of doubt or curiosity. He was asking out of love. Here was a guy who was really getting close to God's heart, and he just wanted to know what his Friend looked like. It was a touching request that must have really moved God. But God's response is equally as moving.

First He explains the hard reality:

You cannot see my face, for no one may see me and live (Exodus 33:20).

But then, out of a tender love and compassion for His friend, God comes up with a solution.

There is a place near me where you may stand on a rock. When my glory passes by, I will put you in a cleft in the rock and cover you with my hand until I have passed by. Then I will remove my hand and you will see my back; but my face must not be seen (Exodus 33:21–23).

What a perfect picture—a perfect blending of God's holiness and His love.

God's Love

"God is love." We've all heard it a million times, and it's definitely biblical. But since the word *love* is tossed around so carelessly these days, let's see what it really means when it refers to God.

PATIENCE

> He is not easily angered; he is full of kindness, and anxious not to punish you (Joel 2:13, TLB).

MERCY AND GRACE

> But God is so rich in mercy; he loved us so much that even though we were spiritually dead and doomed by our sins, he gave us back our lives again when he raised Christ from the dead—only by his undeserved favor have we ever been saved—and lifted us up from the grave into glory along with Christ, where we sit with him in the heavenly realms—all because of what Christ Jesus did (Ephesians 2:4–6, TLB)

FAITHFULNESS

The Old Testament hero Joshua spent an entire lifetime trusting God. As Joshua prepared to die, he had this to say about God's unfailing faithfulness:

> You know with all your heart and soul that not one of all the good promises the LORD your God gave you has failed. Every promise has been fulfilled; not one has failed (Joshua 23:14).

And the Lord himself gave this promise:

> The heavens will vanish like smoke, the earth will wear out like a garment and its inhabitants die like flies. But my salvation will last forever, my righteousness will never fail (Isaiah 51:6).

PROTECTOR AND DEFENDER

"For the eyes of the Lord are on the righteous and his ears are attentive to their prayer, but the face of the Lord is against those who do evil." Who is going to harm you if you are eager to do good? (1 Peter 3:12–13).

Are not two sparrows sold for a penny? Yet not one of them will fall to the ground apart from the will of your Father. And even the very hairs of your head are all numbered. So don't be afraid; you are worth more than many sparrows (Matthew 10:29–31).

PROVIDER

So do not worry, saying, "What shall we eat?" or "What shall we drink?" or "What shall we wear?" For the pagans run after all these things, and your heavenly Father knows that you need them. But seek first his kingdom and his righteousness, and all these things will be given to you as well (Matthew 6:31–33).

GUIDE

The LORD will guide you always (Isaiah 58:11).

SAVIOR

For God so loved the world that he gave his one and only Son, that whoever believes in him shall not perish but have eternal life. For God did not send his Son into the world to condemn the world, but to save the world through him (John 3:16–17).

Tougher Qualities

But God's no wimp. There's a tougher side to Him too. Qualities such as . . .

WRATH

Wrath can be defined as "justifiable anger." And if anyone's got a right to be hot under the collar, I figure it's God. I mean, look how people treat Him, His commands, His world, and His loved ones.

Because of His mercy and patience, He's been holding back His wrath. But it won't be that way forever. The apostle John, who took a sight-seeing tour into heaven and the future, put what he saw this way:

> Then the kings of the earth, the princes, the generals, the rich, the mighty, and every slave and every free man hid in caves and among the rocks of the mountains. They called to the mountains and the rocks, "Fall on us and hide us from the face of him who sits on the throne and from the wrath of the Lamb [Jesus]! For the great day of their wrath has come, and who can stand?" (Revelation 6:15–17).

JEALOUSY

And for those who think God really doesn't care who you worship, there are these words:

> Do not worship any other god, for the LORD, whose name is Jealous, is a jealous God (Exodus 34:14).

> They made him jealous with their foreign gods and angered him with their detestable idols (Deuteronomy 32:16).

The Trinity

Finally, no discussion about God can be complete without mentioning the Trinity. Over and over again the Scriptures make it clear that "the Lord is one" (Deuteronomy 6:4). OK, fine, no problem.

But there are plenty of other Scriptures that talk

about the Holy Spirit being God, about Jesus Christ being God, and about the Father being God. So what gives? How many do we have here? Will the real God please stand up?

It's true, we do have one God. But He exists in three distinct Persons. Confusing? You bet. We don't have anything in our own human experience to compare Him with. But the Scriptures clearly identify these three Persons—just as clearly as they tell us that God is one.

> Let *us* make man in *our* image, in *our* likeness (Genesis 1:26, italics added).

> Therefore go and make disciples of all nations, baptizing them in the name of the *Father* and of the *Son* and of the *Holy Spirit*. Matthew 28:19 (italics added).

In fact, all three Persons of the Trinity made a special appearance (or at least were heard) on the occasion of Jesus' baptism:

> As soon as Jesus was baptized, he went up out of the water. At that moment heaven was opened, and he saw the Spirit of God descending like a dove and lighting on him. And a voice from heaven said, "This is my Son, whom I love; with him I am well pleased" (Matthew 3:16–17).

The Best Picture

If you're having problems putting together all that I've said about God, then just go ahead and picture Jesus Christ.

> He is the image of the invisible God, the first-born over all creation. For by him all things were created: things in heaven and on earth,

29

visible and invisible . . . . all things were created by him and for him. He is before all things, and in him all things hold together. . . . For God was pleased to have *all* his fullness dwell in him'' (Colossians 1:15–17, 19).

CHAPTER 3

Why Do Good People Suffer?

was barely out of high school when my folks told me that they were getting a divorce. Talk about emotional devastation. I was a wreck. Our home was split apart, the love and security of my family was ripped away, even the house we had built on property that we had cleared with our own hands was eventually sold to total strangers. Suddenly everything in my life that seemed safe and good was gone.

Well, almost everything. At least I had the girl I'd dated for three years and was planning on marrying. Amidst all of the turmoil, I knew I could still count on her. She was my only security and the only thing I had left. Then, less than six weeks after my folks broke their news, she had some news of her own—she was in love with another guy.

I have never experienced such pain, such anguish. Hit me with a car, give me a couple of broken arms—physical pain would have been a blessing compared to the emotional torment I was going through. (Of course now, when I look back, this seems like small potatoes compared to world hunger or terminal cancer, but you couldn't have convinced me of that then.) I remember the hurt was so intense that there were times I could barely breathe. I remember begging God to take the pain away or, better yet, to take my life. And through the tears, the sleeplessness, and the aimless wanderings in the middle of the night, I kept asking the question, WHY?

*What have I done to deserve this? I haven't killed any-
body, haven't robbed any banks, haven't beaten up any babies.
I mean, I'm a Christian, for crying out loud! So why, why, if
You love me, are You torturing me???*

It took nearly 15 years, but I finally found my answer.

Why Pain?

In his excellent book *Where Is God When it Hurts?*
Philip Yancey insists that some types of pain are a gift.
And he's right. Without pain we wouldn't know if our
hand was resting on a hot stove (until we started smell-
ing smoke). Without pain we might keep hammering
our thumb instead of the nail. Without pain we
wouldn't even know if there was something wrong with
our body that needed fixing.

And in case you still think life without pain would
be some sort of gift from heaven, Yancey goes on to describe a condition where people are actually "blessed"
with such a gift, where they actually lose the ability to
feel pain. Its name? Leprosy.

When leprosy strikes, parts of the body go numb. I
used to think that all those fingerless hands and leg
stumps were because leprosy had rotted off those parts
of the body. Not true. Those parts had simply lost their
ability to feel pain. And, over the years, the victims had
slowly worn out, infected, or broken them off. Why?
Because they didn't know they were injuring those
parts. They no longer had any type of warning system.
They no longer could feel pain.

For them, this inability to feel pain was no blessing.
Instead, it was a terrible curse.

But Does Pain Have to Hurt?

Philip Yancey talks about various warning systems
that doctors have tried to use in place of pain. You

know, systems that would stimulate other senses instead of our pain center—senses like sight or hearing. But the results were ineffective:

> The signal was not unpleasant enough. A patient would tolerate a loud noise if he wanted to do something such as turn a screwdriver too hard, even though the signal told him it could be harmful [to his hand]. Blinking lights were tried and eliminated for the same reason. Brand [the head doctor] finally resorted to electric shock to make people let go of something that might hurt them. People had to be *forced* to remove their hands. . . . The stimulus had to be unpleasant, just as pain is unpleasant (*Where Is God When It Hurts?* [Zondervan], p. 28).

So in many ways pain is actually a type of gift. Without it, we would literally destroy our bodies.

What About Other Types of Suffering?

Hunger, disease, war, murders—what about that type of stuff?

First, keep in mind that these types of suffering were not in God's original plan. Remember the Garden of Eden with all its happiness? That's what He originally intended for us—not the pain, suffering, and death we have today.

But because we insisted on doing things our way, we invited sin into this world, and with sin came all its pain, suffering, and death. Suffering is a natural result and warning sign that something is wrong with our world (sin) just as physical pain is a natural result and warning sign that something is wrong with our body.

Without sin there would only be love and respect—no violence, no murders, no war.

Without sin there would be enough love and sharing so nobody would be starving or in need.

Without the abuse of sin on our bodies they would never have become so vulnerable to sickness and disease.

And without sin, God would not have had to introduce death. (Although it's a judgment, He also introduced it as a relief so we wouldn't have to endure the sufferings of our sinful world for eternity.)

But couldn't God have made us so we wouldn't sin?

Sure. He could have made us into mindless little robots that would always love Him and always do exactly what He said. But the only problem is that we wouldn't have any freedom. We'd have no choice. We'd be like some battery-powered doll that, whenever you pressed the button, would automatically say, "I love you."

What a joke. That's not love. And love is what God wants—a real, honest-to-goodness love relationship, not some programmed computer response. God wants us to love Him because *we* want to love Him—plain and simple. If He wanted mindless wind-up toys, He would have created them.

But Why Does It Happen to Good People?

There is probably no more haunting question in the world than this one. In the Old Testament the entire book of Job is devoted to this one thought. Let's take a look at what it says:

The Bible calls Job "the greatest man among the people of the East." In fact, on more than one occasion God himself referred to Job as "blameless and upright, a man who fears God and shuns evil" (Job 1:8, 2:3). And yet God allowed Satan to destroy all of Job's livestock (11,000 head), his servants, every one of his 10 children, and to strike down Job himself with painful boils from head to foot.

Talk about intense. But why? What did Job do to deserve such suffering? Was it because, as his friends kept suggesting, he was being punished for something he did wrong? Hardly. God himself said Job was blameless.

So what gives? Was God trying to teach him something?

If He was, He never bothered telling Job.

Was He trying to get Job to work up a bunch of faith so he could get healed?

Nope. According to the Bible, the guy already loved and believed God with his whole heart.

Was it because God had forgotten?

No way. Chapters 1 and 2 are full of God's talking about the guy.

So why?

Again, the answer comes back to God's wanting sincere love.

Satan kept telling God that He wasn't really giving Job a choice. He kept saying that the only reason Job loved the Lord was because He kept blessing him. In essence he accused God of buying Job's love—instead of giving the man a free choice to make up his own mind.

What was the Lord's response to Satan? "Do with him as you please, only spare his life" (Job 2:6, TLB). And Satan did just that!

I wonder how often in our own suffering God is simply purifying our love for Him. How often is He proving to us and the rest of the universe that our love for Him doesn't have to depend on things or circumstances or on getting our own way? True love is not something that has to be bribed or bought; it can become something that is true and deep and eternal—no matter what happens.

Other Reasons

Besides purifying our love, there are three other reasons that God allows good people to suffer.

TO DISCIPLINE US

> Our fathers disciplined us for a little while as
> they thought best; but God disciplines us for
> our good, that we may share in his holiness.
> No discipline seems pleasant at the time, but
> painful. Later on, however, it produces a har-
> vest of righteousness and peace for those who
> have been trained by it (Hebrews 12:10–11).

I almost hesitate to bring this up since discipline is
the first thing everyone always points to. *I wonder why
that happened to so-and-so? He must really be out of line. Or,
God, why are you doing this to me? What am I doing that's
so wrong?*

It's true that if there's something out of sync in your
life God may indeed be using some form of trial or
hardship to get your attention and let you know He's
not fooling around. And, like the pain from touching a
hot stove, it may not be pleasant—for the time being.
But in the long run you'll be happier for a little pain
now than for burning flesh later.

But remember: this is only one of several ways the
Lord uses suffering. Be *very careful* not to jump to this
conclusion too often about yourself—and especially
about other people.

TO COMFORT OTHERS

Another reason we suffer is so we can help others
who have or will be going through similar situations. As
the apostle Paul said to his friends,

> If we are distressed, it is for your comfort and
> salvation; if we are comforted, it is for your
> comfort (2 Corinthians 1:6).

It's one thing to cruise up in your limo to a suffering
person, roll down your tinted glass window, and shout,
"Hey, where's your faith, scum? If you really believed,

God would help you." But it's quite another to be down there in the mud and mire with the writhing and hopeless and saying, "Yes, I know how much you ache; I know how impossible it seems; I was there. But hang on, man; Jesus will be here any minute to help. He did it for me and I know He'll do it for you."

Just as Jesus came down from heaven to participate in our sufferings, it shouldn't come as too big a surprise that we are called to participate in the sufferings of others.

TO MAKE US COMPLETE, LACKING NOTHING

This is the final and perhaps most important reason we suffer.

> Consider it pure joy, my brothers, whenever you face trials of many kinds, because you know that the testing of your faith develops perseverance. Perseverance must finish its work so that you may be mature and complete, not lacking anything (James 1:2–4).

I doubt there's a one of us who feels totally "complete" and "not lacking anything." And for good reason—we're not. Sin's taken quite a toll on our lives. I guess you could say that, one way or another, we're all walking around with crippled souls. But God, the great therapist, loves us too much to let us hobble around forever. He works with us, He forces us to take that extra step, to run that extra lap, to do that extra pull-up—no matter how painful it may seem.

Why? Because of His love. Because, like a dedicated coach who pushes us to the limit to strengthen us and make us winners, God will use our sufferings as a training tool to make us whole, to turn us into everything we can possibly be—to make us "mature and complete, not lacking anything."

Like a good coach, He wants what's best for us, even

though we may not see it at the moment. Without the pain there would be no gain.

The disciple Peter puts it another way:

> So be truly glad! There is wonderful joy ahead, even though the going is rough for a while down here. These trials are only to test your faith, to see whether or not it is strong and pure. It is being tested as fire tests gold and purifies it—and your faith is more precious to God than mere gold; so if your faith remains strong after being tried in the test tube of fiery trials, it will bring you much praise and glory and honor on the day of his return (1 Peter 1:6–7, TLB).

You see, in the old days when they used to smelt and purify gold, they would heat it up until the impurities in the ore surfaced. Then they'd scrape the worthless stuff off and heat up the remaining gold again . . . then again . . . and again—each time making the metal purer and purer.

And how did the refiner know when to stop? When he was able to look into the ore and see a perfect reflection of himself.

That's what God wants.

> For from the very beginning God decided that those who came to him . . . should become like his Son (Romans 8:29, TLB).

Jesus is the perfect example of being a whole, complete human being. He is the perfect example of being "mature and complete, not lacking anything." And, for our own happiness, that's what God wants for us. The purifying may not be pleasant, but it's definitely necessary.

The Real Question Is "How?" Not "Why?"

Although some pain was invented by God to protect us (like the pain from touching a hot stove), most of it has been invented or brought on by ourselves when we introduced sin into the world.

Yet, because "in all things God works for the good of those who love him" (Romans 8:28), He will take this terrible, hellish invention of ours and, if we love Him, somehow use it for our good. We may not see it right away. In fact, we may *never* see it. God never did tell Job why (although before Job's life was over God gave him nearly double of everything the devil had destroyed).

But that shouldn't matter. Our question shouldn't be "Why?" it should be "How?" *How* can I use this to become everything You want me to be? *How* can I use this to draw closer to You? *How* can I use this to serve others better?

There is a world of difference between these two words. "Why?" is questioning, fighting, and doubting. "How?" is accepting whatever God has in mind and moving on to all that He wants us to be. Asking "How?" instead of "Why?" isn't easy. But it's always best.

Oh, one last thing. Remember all that emotional pain I went through just out of high school? Well, as a *direct* result of all that hurt, I gave up the 20 percent of my life that I was holding back from the Lord. And because of that commitment, I changed my major in college, married a wonderful wife, have great kids, and travel all over the world writing and directing films—experiencing some pretty incredible adventures that I would never have even dreamed possible.

All of this because He loved me enough to allow me to suffer.

And all of this because I eventually stopped asking "Why?" and started asking "How?"

CHAPTER 4

Sex—If You Love Someone, Why Not?

've known all my life that the Bible condemns sex outside of marriage. But I've never known why. I mean, I had a few lame excuses in case anyone dared ask—but deep inside I never really understood why. Why, in this day and age with birth control and "safe sex" and everything, is God still so down on premarital sex?

It made for some rather interesting conversations when kids would come to me for counsel. I mean, I could rattle off all the Bible verses I wanted, but if they continued to push me I could only come up with something as profound as, "Well, God says no because, well, uh . . . because He says no."

Great logic.

Now, it's true if God says no then that should settle it. We may never understand all of His ways and reasons, but if He says it then we should obey it. Still, it doesn't hurt to check into His logic from time to time and see what He's up to, to see how He's looking out for us.

First let's look at *what* He says, and then *why*.

God's Word

In case there's any doubt about God's feelings, here are just a few verses of what He has to say about sex outside of marriage:

> If . . . no proof of the girl's virginity can be found, she shall be brought to the door of her father's house and there the men of her

town shall stone her to death (Deuteronomy 22:20–21).

If a man is found sleeping with another man's wife, both the man who slept with her and the woman must die (Deuteronomy 22:22).

If a man happens to meet in a town a virgin pledged to be married and he sleeps with her, you shall take both of them to the gate of that town and stone them to death (Deuteronomy 22:23–24).

And take a look at the company God puts the sexually immoral with. . . .

For out of the heart come evil thoughts, murder, adultery, sexual immorality, theft, false testimony, slander (Matthew 15:19).

Do not be deceived: Neither the sexually immoral nor idolaters nor adulterers nor male prostitutes nor homosexual offenders nor thieves nor the greedy nor drunkards nor slanderers nor swindlers will inherit the kingdom of God (1 Corinthians 6:9–10).

But the cowardly, the unbelieving, the vile, the murderers, the sexually immoral, those who practice magic arts, the idolaters and all liars—their place will be in the fiery lake of burning sulfur. This is the second death (Revelation 21:8).

There's more, but I think you get the idea. So the bottom line is pretty obvious: God's answer to sex outside of marriage is a not so subtle *"No way!!!"* Whether it's backseat gymnastics or the ol' "Let's live together first just to make sure," God's response is always the same. No matter how we try to rationalize it, it always comes up *"No sale."*
WHY?

What's the reason? Is it too enjoyable? Is God a prude? Is He really out to make sure we don't have a good time?

I know I sound like a broken record, but keep in mind that God's ultimate goal is for us to be "mature and complete, not lacking anything" (James 1:4). Keep in mind that Jesus came so we "might have life, and might have it abundantly" (John 10:10, NASB). So somehow, some way, holding off on sex until we're married is for our own good.

Here are a few reasons. . . .

1. PREGNANCY

Even with all the contraceptives on the market, the rate of unwanted pregnancies among teens is sky-high. In fact, according to Dr. Ray E. Short, a professor of sociology, in his book *Sex, Dating, and Love* (Augsburg), "One out of three teens who has sex gets pregnant outside of marriage." *One out of three.* He goes on to mention that "one in five of these gets pregnant within the first month after she starts having sex" (p. 82).

Not great odds. And the scariest thing is I doubt any of those teens ever dreamed it would happen to them.

But what about birth control?

Condoms fail 10–15% of the time. That's a lot!

And the pill? According to Family Planning Perspectives 9–18% of unmarried teens on the pill become pregnant during their first year of using it. That's even more!

2. DISEASE

Currently there are 20–25 different types of sexually transmitted diseases (STDs). Some have no cure. Others can kill, maim, and leave you unable to have children.

There's even scarier news. At the moment one out of every five Americans between the ages of 15 and 25 is infected with a viral STD. One out of five! And the sad thing is many of them don't even know it.

And what about AIDS?

The number of teens with AIDS doubles every 14 months.

According to the Institute for Sexual Health, AIDS was the leading cause of death of persons aged 24–44.

But what about Safe Sex?

Unfortunately there is no such thing. If condoms fail 10–15% of the time in controlling pregnancy, their number is EVEN HIGHER with STDs and AIDS. Why? "The germs that cause STDs are *much* smaller than sperm, so they're more likely to escape from a condom through a small hole or tear. The diameter of the virus that causes AIDS is 1/25 the diameter of sperm" (Joe S. McIlhaney Jr., M.D., *Why Condoms Aren't Safe* [Focus on the Family]).

These are the obvious, more visible dangers. But there are plenty of invisible ones. . . .

3. RELATIONSHIP WITH EACH OTHER

Sex between husband and wife is the deepest, most intimate form of communication and giving. When properly expressed it draws them closer and helps to form that lifelong bond of "becoming one."

But outside of marriage, it has just the opposite effect, often separating the very ones that are using it to draw together. In fact, according to Dr. Short, "The couple who gets involved in premarital sex is less likely to marry each other than if they stay virgins" (p. 71).

At first glance this may seem strange. But keep in mind that since "physical love" is a lot easier (and more fun) to express, it often replaces the more difficult but more essential elements so necessary to build a real and lasting relationship. Elements such as honest communication, devoted friendship, sharing of fears, hopes, expectations, the ability to become transparent, vulnerable. . . . Sadly, these building blocks are just passed over for the easier, more self-gratifying "roll in the hay." And, as a result, the deeper bonds are never built.

Then there's the matter of trust—the very cornerstone of a lasting relationship. But the same sex that helps bind and seal trust in a marriage can cause tremendous doubt and suspicion among unmarrieds. . . . "If she did it with me, what's to stop her from doing it with others?"

Finally there is the spiritual side of things. If a Christian couple is seriously considering a deeper relationship, it's a must that they also grow and develop on a spiritual level. But if they're having sex and know God disapproves—I mean, let's face it—their chances of growing together spiritually won't be so hot.

These are just some of the reasons that premarital sex actually destroys the very relationship the couple is trying to build.

Then there is the matter of . . .

4. RELATIONSHIP WITH GOD

We've just touched on this one. But sin always, *always* eats away at our relationship with God. We can pray until there are blisters on our knees, but we'll always feel alone and cut off from God until we stop and repent.

5. RELATIONSHIP WITH FUTURE MATE

Of all the damage that can happen from premarital sex, I think this is the worst. Those who get into sex before they get married often have a difficult time enjoying sex once they do get married.

Why?

They've built a barrier that prevents them from giving themselves entirely to their mate. They've learned to hold back and not completely lose themselves in the act. It's a type of protection, of emotional survival from times past—when there was the unspoken fear of whether he or she would really be there the next morning, the next week, the next year.

Unfortunately that mental pattern may take years to break. In fact, I know at least one person who took nearly ten years before finally being able to give fully to their mate and totally enjoy sex. Talk about a rip-off.

Then, of course, there is the matter of comparison. *Am I really as good as he or she had in the past? Maybe if I just work a little harder . . .*

Sex shouldn't be something we have to work at. It's not a performance. But for many, that most intimate time of affection and communion is ruined by the "Comparison Factor": *Is she really as good as what's-her-name? Am I really as good as that other guy?*

Unfortunately all this information is not manufactured by some religious fanatic trying to justify what the Bible says. It's supported by cold, hard scientific evidence. Once again here are some of the findings compiled by Professor Short in his book *Sex, Dating, and Love* (pp. 71–72).

- "Nonvirgins tend to have less happy marriages than virgins."
- "Nonvirgins are more apt to split up or be divorced after marriage than virgins."
- "Persons who have had premarital sex are more likely to cheat on their spouse (commit adultery) after they are married."
- "While those with previous sex experience say they do *adjust quicker* in their sex life after the wedding . . . the virgins are *more happy with their total sex life* in marriage than the nonvirgins."
- "Nonvirgins often get trapped into poor marriages by 'flunking the test of time.' Their good sex life fools them into thinking they have a good total adjustment when they do not. They marry and soon wish they had not."
- "The guilt, fear, and low self-regard that is felt in

premarital sex will carry over and help spoil the sex life of the pair after marriage."

Why the Urge?

If sex before marriage is so wrong, so harmful, then why do I have to deal with the desire now, before there's anything I can do about it?

A good question. And the answer doesn't lie in everybody running out and getting married at 14. The truth is those desires don't go away even when you do get married. They're still there, nagging away, whispering in the back of your mind. There's always somebody better looking, sexier, more enticing.

So why the urge?

Sex is a desire—a strong desire. In many ways it's no different from, say, hunger. By itself, there is nothing wrong with hunger. It's a perfectly natural and healthy desire . . . as long as I keep it in control. But if I were to go on an eating binge and put away a dozen Big Macs at the local arches, I'd have a problem. I'd no longer be controlling my appetite; it would be controlling me.

The same is true with sex. As long as I control it I'm in good shape. But as soon as it starts to control me I'm in trouble. So it's no big surprise that the Lord uses the battleground of sex as one of the main tools in developing the mega-important gift for His kids of *self-control*.

Self-control: one of the most important gifts. With it you can master your entire life; without it you're like a ship tossed and thrown by every whim and fancy— no direction, no purpose. With self-control, both in your thought life and actions, your life will have meaning and direction. Without it life is basically worthless.

So the next time those desires come, try to look on them as an opportunity to grow, as an opportunity to be in control. And as you continue to develop in this area you'll be able to master nearly every other area of your life.

Lust Busting

It's not always *easy* to overcome lust, but it is always *possible*.

> And God is faithful; he will not let you be tempted beyond what you can bear. But when you are tempted, he will also provide a way out so that you can stand up under it (1 Corinthians 10:13).

Remember, the battle is never won or lost below the belt—it's always won or lost in the mind. Fleeting thoughts come and go; that's only natural. It's when we ask them to stay, when we start to dwell on them, that we get into trouble. In fact, as soon as we decide "to dwell," we can kiss victory good-bye.

The solution?

> Take captive every thought to make it obedient to Christ (2 Corinthians 10:5).

Martin Luther referred to lust as birds flitting about a tree. If they try to land, the tree has only to shake them off. But if the tree allows them to stay, before it knows it, a whole family of birds have built their nests and are hatching their young.

Since the battle is won or lost in the mind, it's important to feed that mind with the Lord's ammunition, not the devil's. Stay away from the lusty books, magazines, movies, TV shows—anything that gives the enemy weapons to attack. It's tough, I know. But it is possible. Instead:

> Whatever is true, whatever is honorable, whatever is right, whatever is pure, whatever is lovely, whatever is of good repute, if there is

any excellence and if anything worthy of
praise, let your mind dwell on these things
(Philippians 4:8, NASB).

In short, give the Lord His fair share of the ammunition.

It's true, lust can cause a pretty intense war inside
the head. But as you keep saying yes to what God
would have you think and no to what the world keeps
trying to make you think, it becomes easier and easier
to resist temptation.

Stacy and Paula Rinehart, in their excellent book
Choices (NavPress, p. 103), put it best:

> As Christians, our lives are like a two-track
> model train; one track represents life in the
> Spirit, while the other represents life in the
> flesh. The train can't run on both tracks si-
> multaneously. The question is, to which track
> will you throw the power switch *on?* When
> you choose to allow your spiritual drive to
> dominate and energize you, the desires of the
> flesh go dormant. Your train will run in the
> power of the Spirit, exhibiting the Spirit's
> fruit—self-control. Moment by moment, you
> must decide which track will have the power.
>
> Whichever drive you feed the most will
> control you. If you know that certain friends,
> books, records, activities, or manners of dress
> energize your physical drive, steer clear of
> those influences. If you acknowledge that the
> Word and genuine Christian fellowship acti-
> vate the power of the Spirit, then cultivate
> those habits and watch self-control take root
> and bloom afresh.

The choice is always yours.

Repentance and Forgiveness

And if you've already had or are practicing sex, what then? Are you scarred and wounded for life? Damned for eternity?

Again, the decision is yours.

Jesus makes it clear that if we confess and return to Him, "He is faithful and just and will forgive us our sins" (1 John 1:9)—tossing them into His "sea of forgetfulness," separating them from us "as far as the East is from the West," making us "whiter than snow." I mean, that was the whole purpose of His dying on the cross. So if we repent, if we turn from our sin and ask for forgiveness, in His mind it's as if the sin had never happened. Not a bad deal, and as always, it's available to anyone who asks.

But I'd be lying if I said each person that did this would instantaneously be healed of all the emotional scars and damage such sin may have caused.

Sometimes that's the case. Sometimes not. Wounds often take time to heal. But with Jesus' help they do heal. And the sooner a person turns from sin and gets his act together, the sooner God can start His work.

All this to say . . .

Sex is a wonderful experience when enjoyed in marriage as God intended it. It can be the most intimate and personal form of communion between two people.

But when it's used outside of His intentions, it robs and destroys on every front—physically, emotionally, and spiritually.

CHAPTER 5

Is There a Heaven?

veryone likes to believe there's a heaven. You know, the place where all us good folk go and finally get our goodies—that big awards assembly in the sky.

But what is heaven really like? And to be more honest, how do we know it really exists? Could we just be fooling ourselves with a little wishful thinking? Where's the proof?

Good questions. Let's see if there are some answers.

Jesus Believed

For starters, Jesus believed there is a heaven.

Rejoice and be glad, because great is your reward in heaven (Matthew 5:12).

In fact, He made it pretty clear that He considered heaven home base:

Father, glorify me in your presence with the glory I had with you before the world began (John 17:5).

He also made it pretty clear that that's where He was going:

In my Father's house are many rooms; if it were not so, I would have told you. I am going there to prepare a place for you. And if I go and prepare a place for you, I will come back and take you to be with me that you also may be where I am (John 14:2–3).

And finally, He wasted no words telling us that the only way for us to get there is *through* Him:

> I am the way and the truth and the life. No one comes to the Father except through me (John 14:6).

So as far as Jesus was concerned, there was definitely a heaven, a place where people who put their trust in Him would go.

What's It Like?

In the book of Revelation, the apostle John recounts his quick tour of the place. This is *some* of what he saw:

> In a vision he took me to a towering mountain peak and from there I watched that wondrous city, the holy Jerusalem, descending out of the skies from God. It was filled with the glory of God, and flashed and glowed like a precious gem, crystal clear like jasper.
>
> When he [the angel tour guide] measured it, he found it was a square as wide as it was long; in fact it was in the form of a cube, for its height was exactly the same as its other dimensions—1,500 miles each way.
>
> The city itself was pure, transparent gold like glass! The wall was made of jasper, and was built on twelve layers of foundation stones inlaid with gems.
>
> Nothing evil will be permitted in it—no one immoral or dishonest—but only those whose names are written in the Lamb's Book of Life.
>
> And He pointed out to me a river of pure Water of Life, clear as crystal, flowing from the throne of God and the Lamb, coursing down the center of the main street (Revelation

21:10–11, 16, 18–19, 27; 22:1–2, TLB).

And this is only *part* of what He saw.

But you know, descriptions of heaven aren't just in the Bible (though that should be enough). Reliable witnesses who, through modern medicine, have died and been brought back to life again also believe they've seen this "celestial city." And although we have to be careful never to take any personal account as seriously as we do the Holy Word of God, and that sometimes Satan can create masterful counterfeits, it's interesting that many people have given exactly the same description.

Here are just a few of numerous eyewitness accounts.

> And then I saw, infinitely far off, far too distant to be visible with any kind of sight I knew of . . . a city. A glowing . . . city, bright enough to be seen over all the unimaginable distance between. The lightness seemed to shine from the very walls and streets of this place, and from beings which I could now discern moving about within it. In fact, the city and everything in it seemed to be made of light (George G. Ritchie with Elizabeth Sherrill, *Return from Tomorrow* [Spire Books], p. 72).

> I noticed I was crossing over a beautiful city below, as I followed the river like a soaring bird. The streets seemed to be made of shining gold and were wonderfully beautiful. I can't describe it. I descended into one of the streets and people were all around me—happy people who were glad to see me! They seemed to be in shining clothes with a sort of glow (Maraca Rawlings, M.D., *Beyond Death's Door* [Bantam Books], p. 76).

> As I approached him I felt a great reverence and I asked him, "Are you Jesus?"
> He said, "No, you will find Jesus and your

loved ones beyond that door." After he looked in his book he said, "You may go on through."

And then I walked through the door, and saw on the other side this beautiful, brilliantly lit city. . . . It was all made of gold or something metal with domes and steeples in beautiful array, and the streets were shining. . . . There were many people all dressed in glowing white robes with radiant faces. They looked beautiful *(Beyond Death's Door*, p. 80).

But there's another interesting similarity between what John saw and what some of those who feel they've seen heaven can recall. Remember 1 Timothy 6:15–16, where God is described as so holy that He lives in this "unapproachable light"? In nearly every account there's mention of an incredibly bright being—whose very presence seems to light the city—somebody whom everyone seems to be worshiping.

His face was like the sun shining in all its brilliance (Revelation 1:16).

I saw that it was not light but a Man . . . a man made out of light, though this seemed no more possible to my mind than the incredible intensity of the brightness that made up His form *(Return from Tomorrow*, pp. 48–49).

No temple could be seen in the city, for the Lord God Almighty and the Lamb [Jesus] are worshiped in it everywhere. And the city has no need of sun or moon to light it, for the glory of God and the Lamb illuminate it (Revelation 21:22–23, TLB).

What Does it Feel Like?

Most people describe heaven or their experience of standing in front of Jesus as an intense love and breathtaking awe. It's as if all of the worries and troubles of the world suddenly mean nothing when compared to what they see. The only thing that matters is the love and awesome power they experience radiating from Jesus Christ.

> The instant I perceived Him, a command formed itself in my mind. "Stand up!" The words came from inside me, yet they had an authority my mere thoughts had never had. I got to my feet, and as I did came the stupendous certainty: "You are in the presence of *the* Son of God."
>
> Again, the concept seemed to form itself inside me, but not as thought or speculation. It was a kind of knowing, immediate and complete. . . . If this was *the* Son of God, then His name was Jesus. But . . . this was not the Jesus of my Sunday School books. That Jesus was gentle, kind, understanding—and probably a little bit of a weakling. This Person was power itself, older than time and yet more modern than anyone I had ever met.
>
> Above all, with that same mysterious inner certainty, I knew that this Man loved me. Far more even than the power, what emanated from this Presence was unconditional love. An astonishing love. A love beyond my wildest imagining. This love knew every unlovable thing about me—the quarrels with my stepmother, my explosive temper, the sex thoughts I could never control, every mean, selfish thought and action since the day I was born— and accepted and loved me just the same (*Return from Tomorrow*, p. 49).

Billy Graham, in his book on dying, describes what he believes heaven to "feel" like:

> Have you ever watched young couples in love

communicate without words? Have you been in love yourself? People deeply in love find absolute bliss in each other's presence and wish their moments together would go on forever. If those moments could be frozen, with no sense of passing time, would that be "heaven" for them? . . .

I suspect those feelings are a small indication of what it would be like, frozen in time and loving God, enjoying Him, forever (*Facing Death and the Life After* [Word Books], p. 223).

These are great descriptions. But remember, they are only personal experiences or opinions. And both can sometimes be wrong or be counterfeited. The real proof lies in what the Bible teaches:

Now the dwelling of God is with men, and he will live with them. They will be his people, and God himself will be with them and be their God. He will wipe every tear from their eyes. There will be no more death or mourning or crying or pain (Revelation 21:3–4).

Sounds pretty good to me!

The point is, if Jesus left earth to prepare a place for us in heaven, chances are it must be pretty awesome.

Or, as the Bible puts it:

No eye has seen, no ear has heard, no mind has conceived what God has prepared for those who love him (1 Corinthians 2:9).

How Do We Get There?

No discussion of heaven would be complete without mentioning how we get there. Despite the rumors, we don't get there through good works, or through being super religious, or even by going to church every Sunday.

As Jesus said, there's one way and one way only—through Him.

> For God so loved the world that he gave his one and only Son, that whoever believes in him shall not perish but have eternal life. For God did not send his Son into the world to condemn the world, but to save the world through him (John 3:16–17).

CHAPTER 6

How Can I Make God More Real in My Life?

Not long ago I was filming a preacher who was visiting New York. He had scheduled an outdoor crusade in one of the more hostile parks of the city. It was a gutsy move, but he had a reputation for being a gutsy man. However, this time it looked like all the preparation was going to be in vain. A tremendous thunderstorm was rolling in, complete with dark, churning clouds and enough wind to make even Dorothy and Toto nervous. Already people were packing up and running for cover. But not the preacher.

Standing off to one side he was quietly rebuking the storm, forbidding it to come over the crusade. And you know what? It didn't. The rain poured everywhere else, but not in that little park. Everywhere else it blew, it thundered, it flashed. But it did not, it *could* not, rain where we were . . . not until the Gospel had been preached, the altar call made, and the people's needs met. After that it poured!

This sort of miracle happens in his ministry all the time (usually it's people's lives that are miraculously changed, not the weather). And standing there in the wind I couldn't help but think of so many young Christians I know who think their faith is nothing but theory—just a bunch of words. They're nice kids, but so often they believe in God and go to church only because that's what their parents do.

Christianity is not a bunch of words! It is not

something we inherit from our parents! In fact, it isn't even a religion. Christianity is a *relationship*. A relationship with the most powerful and loving Being in the universe! It's not theory. It's action. It's power. It can be an absolute, 100 percent life-changing experience . . . if we want it to be.

Looking for Action?

Check out the disciples. Their lives weren't exactly boring—miracles, healings, raising people from the dead. In fact, it was Jesus himself who said,

> Truly, truly, I say to you, he who believes in me, the works that I do shall he do also; and greater works than these shall he do (John 14:12, NASB).

Now, that sounds anything but boring! Yet so many people just look upon Christianity as a bunch of stories, a bunch of thees and thous, do's and don'ts, with zippo life and zero excitement.

Being a Christian does not have to be a cure for insomnia. There is a whole world out there that is sick and dying. And there's a whole empire of darkness that we can battle and beat.

But even more important, there's a relationship we can experience—a relationship with the Creator of the universe. And believe me, after experiencing and living in a relationship with God Almighty, Christianity becomes anything but a bore!

But how? How do we experience that deeper relationship, that deeper intimacy with God?

A good question. The first step lies in . . .

COMMUNICATION

When it comes right down to it, God requires only one basic thing from us: our love.

> Jesus replied: " 'Love the Lord your God with
> all your heart and with all your soul and with
> all your mind.' This is the first and greatest
> commandment" (Matthew 22:37–38).

But it's impossible to love someone until you get to know him. And it's impossible to get to know someone without . . . communicating. If I were to run out on the street and ask the first girl I met to marry me, she'd probably die laughing. Why? She wouldn't know me, let alone love me. How could we change that? By communicating. She'd talk, I'd listen. I'd talk, she'd listen. And maybe, if we were right for each other, we *might* fall in love.

The same is true between God and us. How can we love Him without really knowing Him? And how can we know Him without communicating—without talking to Him and listening?

Of course the main way we listen to God is by reading His letters to us—His Word. Back in chapter 1 we talked about the importance of reading a little Scripture every day. And we mentioned the strong supernatural power His Word can have in changing our lives—the fact that it actually cleanses (Ephesians 5:26), encourages (Romans 15:4), equips us for *every* good work (2 Timothy 3:16–17), and even gives us faith (Romans 10:17).

But what about this other side of communicating: talking with God?

Everyone has a pretty good idea of what it means to pray. In fact, it's always amazing how "religious" people get when a surprise geometry test is suddenly sprung on them or when they zip past that state trooper at 78 miles per hour. Nearly everyone has thrown out a few "help me, help me's" from time to time. And there's nothing wrong with that. But that's only one side of prayer. There's another, much deeper aspect— one that, if practiced correctly, can draw you into the very heart of God. It's called . . .

Praise

Nothing has changed and empowered my life more than the practice of praise. I don't just mean a quickie "Praise the Lord." I'm talking deep, reverent worship for 5, 10, even 15 minutes. I'm not sure of all that happens. All I know is that every person who practices praising God is eventually brought into deep fellowship and communion with Him. Praise is some sort of key we use to unlock the door and enter into God's presence. In fact, Psalm 100 commands us to enter His presence just that way:

> Enter his gates with thanksgiving and his courts with praise (Psalm 100:4).

Somehow or other, praise brings us more deeply into God's presence. And when you are before God, life is anything but boring.

Sometimes when you're in His presence you may simply feel a deep, silent peace. Another time it may be a warm glow of love or sense of joy. At another time you may feel an impression or word from God specifically for you. There are other times when tears may flow as He touches you with a deeper aspect of His love and goodness. Other times you may get so excited you might want to shout, clap, sing, or even dance before Him. Don't worry about it. If it's for God, if it's a way of worshiping and showing your love and excitement for Him, go for it. (You might want to try it with the shades pulled, but go for it.)

Since praise and worship are so empowering to the believer, you can bet Satan will do all he can to prevent you from connecting into that power. So here are a few hands-on, how-to hints.

PRACTICE PRAISING THE LORD

Set aside a quiet time every day for just you and the Lord. It doesn't have to be long—just 10 or 15 minutes of praise and worship. But watch out. As your life gets more hectic with more demands, you can bet Satan will do everything he can to choke out that period. Don't let him.

These minutes are the *most precious of your life*— they're when your soul is fed, when your spirit is strengthened. This is the time when the very Lord whom you've invited into your heart actually grows and takes over more of your life. It's when you and your Creator commune. Don't let anything or anybody steal it from you.

BEATING THE WANDERING MIND

Because of the fast-lane pace and all the demands thrown at you, it can be pretty tough to stop your mind from wandering. For me this is probably the hardest part about worshiping. But there are ways to beat it.

A lot of times I'll start off by singing—not just any Christian song, but a song that really helps me worship and that tells the Lord how great I think He is. After one or two of these I'll pick a slower, more peaceful song and gradually quiet and silence my mind. Finally, I'm sitting very, very still, just dwelling on some specific goodness of Jesus—His mercy, His love, His faithfulness, His provision, even His name. And almost before I know it I've entered His presence. I'll start to feel His peace, His joy.

Sometimes I'll whisper His praises; sometimes I'll just sit silently basking in His presence. That still doesn't mean my mind won't wander. But when it does I just gently direct it back to the Lord.

Eventually I may pick up my Bible and quietly read a psalm of worship *to Him* slowly, with great feeling. Other times I may sing another hymn, or quietly recite words describing His majesty, or dwell on His holiness or on how good He's been to me. It makes no difference. All that matters is that I'm worshiping and experiencing my Creator.

(Unfortunately, a word has to be said here about the occult. Satan loves to take something good and make a counterfeit of it. He has created entire religions based on people forcing their minds to go blank. That's not what we're talking about. We're talking about entering God's presence by *filling* our minds . . . with His love and goodness.)

Let's face it. There are times you just won't feel like praising. You're grumpy. You're irritable. You feel so out of it that if you tried to tell God you were grateful for *anything*, you'd feel like a world-class liar.

I know what you're talking about. We've all been there. But the strange thing about praise is that it's not based on feelings. That's right. Believe it or not, praise and thanksgiving are based on obedience, *not* feelings. In fact, over and over again Scripture commanded the Jewish people to offer a *"sacrifice* of thanksgiving."

So whether you feel particularly thankful or not, force yourself to give thanks. You're not being a hypocrite. Even if it's through gritted teeth, find something to praise God about (maybe that you've got teeth to grit). The good feelings may not come right away, but if you're faithful, God will be faithful. And eventually, 5, 10, 15 minutes into the worship time, you'll find yourself once again starting to experience His love, His joy, His peace. (And if not, that's OK too. At least you're being obedient, and that in itself is some reward.)

PRAISE EVEN IN BAD TIMES

As a new believer I was never much of a Bible verse memorizer. (I should have been but I wasn't.) Yet there were these two verses I just couldn't seem to get out of my head. Everywhere I looked they popped up. In everything I did they came to mind.

The first was in Romans:

And we know that in all things God works for

the good of those who love him, who have been called according to his purpose (Romans 8:28).

For me the thought was staggering. That meant that everything, every single tiny little thing that happened to me, was somehow for my good. "ALL things" . . . not some things, not most things, but "ALL" things. If I stubbed my toe, then somehow God would use it for my good. If my dog lost at playing tag with the cars on the freeway, still somehow, some way, it would be used for my good. I was amazed.

And then, not much later the second verse came along:

Give thanks in all circumstances, for this is God's will for you in Christ Jesus (1 Thessalonians 5:18).

There was that word again: *all*. It's God's will for me to give thanks in "*all* circumstances."

And when I put those verses together I was hit with an incredible concept: God wanted me to thank Him in *everything* because somehow it would *all* be used for my good!

It seemed amazing. But since it was in the Bible I figured I'd give it a shot.

I started practicing it.

And my life has never been the same.

Every time something terrible has happened—from the theft of our life savings to a death in the family—we have practiced giving thanks to the Lord. And every time, God has eventually taken that situation and turned it around for good. That doesn't mean we thank Him *for* the situation (He didn't bring the attack—Satan did). But we thank Him *in the midst of* the situation—thanking Him that He's in charge, that somehow He'll take the bad and turn it around for good. When we do this, it's as if every kick Satan gives only boosts us closer to heaven.

It's been tough at times, and we've certainly done our share of whining and complaining. But anybody can thank God when things look great. The real blessing to our Lord and the real growth inside each of us happens when we force ourselves *by faith* to thank Him for what we cannot see. When things are totally black and there is no hope, that's the time to literally force ourselves to praise. In fact, it's interesting that in more than one psalm David actually *orders* his soul to give thanks.

That's what we have to do: order ourselves to praise, to thank the Lord for whatever He has in store for us. And frequently the faith released in that little act is just enough to move the mountains and allow God to bless us with something far deeper and richer than we had expected.

The Hardest Part

There is one other thing that we have to keep in mind if we really want to experience God and live in His power. It's the toughest, but the most essential. We have to DIE!

Say what?

That's right. If we really want to experience the Lord and be effective for Him, we have to be willing to die to all our hopes, all our desires, and all our dreams. In short, we have to be willing to die to everything that we are and hope to become.

That doesn't mean He won't bring certain things back to life again. But we have to be *willing* to give them all to Him.

Then stand back. Because if I've learned one thing, it's that you can't out-give God. Plan on Him taking the bad and destroying it and giving you back the good— only a thousand times better! Or, as Jesus said, "pressed down, shaken together and running over" (Luke 6:38).

Giving up and dying can be tough—there's no

doubt about it. The Bible refers to it as the great civil war battling inside our heads. The "old man" (our flesh) wanting to stay alive versus the "new man" (the Jesus-part in us) wanting to take control. And that old man can be so sneaky he'll do anything to stick around . . . even if it means doing "good" works.

But according to Jesus, there's only one place for that old man: the cross.

God's got a plan for us. He wants to use us. And we'll be happier and more content if we let *Him* run our lives instead of trying to do it ourselves.

God needs tools that are sensitive to His hands—tools that move and do what *He* wants them to. A sculptor has no use for a chisel that goes off trying to make a statue on its own. He needs a chisel that will respond to his touch, moving where he moves it.

That doesn't mean everyone has to run off and become preachers or missionaries. What it does mean is you have to say, "Yes, Lord, You're the boss." And if you really mean that (or want to mean that) in every area of your life, every day of your life, then be prepared. Plan on God using you for some great things.

All this to say . . .

Christianity does not have to be boring. If you give your whole life to Him, if you're willing to do whatever He asks . . . then stand back and get ready. You'll be in for the time of your life!

CHAPTER 7

Is Hell for Real?

You keep saying, "God is love, God is love." So tell me, how could this God of love send anybody to some great, eternal barbecue pit?

We've all heard this question a dozen times before (and probably thought it just as often). Let's face it, for many of us hell is an embarrassing subject—definitely uncool (in more ways than one). I mean, unless someone is telling somebody to go there, no one really wants to bring up the subject.

But, as we've said before, God's pretty secure with who He is and isn't too concerned about fitting into what's cool and what's not. He's managed to run the universe without our help and opinions this long, chances are He'll continue to do so for a while longer. And, whether we like it or not, there's most definitely a hell.

> I tell you, my friends, do not be afraid of those who kill the body and after that can do no more. But I will show you whom you should fear: Fear him who, after the killing of the body, has power to throw you into hell. Yes, I tell you, fear him (Luke 12:4–5).
>
> The Son of Man will send out his angels, and they will weed out of his kingdom everything that causes sin and all who do evil. They will throw them into the fiery furnace, where there will be weeping and gnashing of teeth (Matthew 13:41–42).

> It is better for you to lose one part of your body than for your whole body to be thrown into hell (Matthew 5:29).

> You snakes! You brood of vipers! How will you escape being condemned to hell? (Matthew 23:33).

Yes, by these verses (and others), it's a safe guess that God wants us to take this place called hell pretty seriously. In fact, in the New Testament hell is mentioned 12 times. And 11 out of those 12 times it's Jesus who is talking about it.

What's It Like?

First of all, anybody that winds up calling it home will be totally cut off from God. His holiness, His glory, and most important His love—all the things that we've seen in the last chapter which make heaven such a great place—will be completely gone.

> They will be punished with everlasting destruction and shut out from the presence of the Lord and from the majesty of his power (2 Thessalonians 1:9).

Bad news. And with the absence of God comes the absence of His light and the absence of His love, making it a place of "darkness, where there will be weeping and gnashing of teeth" (Matthew 22:13).

Sounds harsh, I know. But if people keep telling God to butt out of their lives, that they want nothing to do with Him, He's eventually going to let them have their way—forever.

PHYSICAL DESCRIPTIONS

Just as John got a tour of heaven when he was inspired to write the Book of Revelation, he also got a glimpse of hell.

When he opened the Abyss, smoke rose from it like the smoke from a gigantic furnace. The sun and sky were darkened by the smoke from the Abyss (Revelation 9:2).

The two of them were thrown alive into the fiery lake of burning sulfur (Revelation 19:20).

If anyone's name was not found written in the book of life, he was thrown into the lake of fire (Revelation 20:15).

Then there's Jesus' parable about the suffering poor man and the greedy rich man:

The time came when the beggar died and the angels carried him to Abraham's side [heaven]. The rich man also died and was buried. In hell, where he was in torment, he looked up and saw Abraham far away, with Lazarus by his side. So he called to him, "Father Abraham, have pity on me and send Lazarus to dip the tip of his finger in water and cool my tongue, because I am in agony in this fire."

But Abraham replied, "Son, remember that in your lifetime you received your good things, while Lazarus received bad things, but now he is comforted here and you are in agony. And besides all this, between us and you a great chasm has been fixed, so that those who want to go from here to you cannot, nor can anyone cross over from there to us (Luke 16:22–26).

OTHER DESCRIPTIONS

But what about all these people who die and come back to life? They always talk about heaven; you never hear them talking about hell.

Not true.

Dr. Maurice Rawlings, in his book *Beyond Death's Door*, tells of a patient whose heart stopped while undergoing tests in his office. Through heart massage the doctor was able to bring him back to life. But not for long. As the doctor kept working on him, trying to insert a pacemaker, the guy kept dying on him. And each time the patient regained consciousness, he screamed, "I am in hell!"

Heart massage can be a painfully brutal experience; many have even had their ribs broken in the process. But instead of pleading for the doctor to stop, as is normally the case, the patient begged him to continue. Of course the doctor was dumbfounded, but there was more.

> I noticed a genuinely alarmed look on his face. He had a terrified look *worse* than the expression seen in death! This patient had a grotesque grimace expressing sheer horror! His pupils were dilated, and he was perspiring and trembling—he looked as if his hair was "on end."
>
> Then still another strange thing happened. He said, "Don't you understand? I am in hell. Each time you quit I go back to hell! Don't let me go back to hell!" (p. 3)

After clinically dying a few more times, the patient began pleading with the doctor for some way to stay out of that horrible place. And although the doctor didn't know much about prayer, he did know something about Jesus Christ. And together the two prayed for Christ to save the patient.

Well, the patient eventually recovered. But when Dr. Rawlings talked to him a few days later, the man didn't remember a thing.

"What hell? I don't recall any hell!"

Rawlings described in detail all that had happened,

but the patient still could not recall a single one of the "unpleasant events." After giving it careful consideration, the doctor's final conclusion was this:

> Apparently the experiences were so frightening, so horrible, so painful that his conscious mind could not cope with them; and they were subsequently suppressed far into his subconscious (p. 5).

This may be one reason so few people who have died and come back to life are able to recall being in hell.

But from the unlucky ones who can remember (and there are quite a few) come descriptions very close to the Bible's:

> I was standing some distance from this burning, turbulent, rolling mass of blue fire. As far as my eyes could see it was just the same. A lake of fire and brimstone. . . . There is no way to escape, no way out. You don't even try to look for one. This is the prison out of which no one can escape except by Divine intervention (Thomas Welch, *Oregon's Amazing Miracle* [Dallas: Christ for the Nations, Inc., 1976], p. 8, as quoted by *Beyond Death's Door*, p. 87).

Awaiting Judgment?

But what about those who deny Christ and still claim they were in heaven—you know, saying they were surrounded by smiling relatives or greeted by some "loving light" at the end of a tunnel?

A good question.

But from the experiences I've read and researched, this is often just the first phase of death. Others who have gone further into the death experience talk about a wall or barrier they eventually come to and cannot cross over. Some talk about waiting in a holding area. If this is the case, then perhaps they really are in heaven, but just in a waiting room where they are received until it's their turn to be judged.

And if that's true, and their names are *not* in Jesus' "Book of Life," imagine how horrific it must be to be yanked away from all the love they're surrounded with and wind up in hell.

Again, keep in mind that these human experiences are not to be considered on the same level as the Scripture. But also keep in mind that both Jesus and the Bible speak quite seriously about this place of eternal punishment, and that anyone whose name is not written in the "Lamb's Book of Life" is heading there.

WHY?

If God is so loving, why would He want to send anyone there?

First of all, God doesn't want to send anybody to hell.

> He is patient with you, not wanting anyone to perish, but everyone to come to repentance (2 Peter 3:9).

He wants so desperately for us to stay out of the place that He came down from heaven and suffered and died the most agonizing and humiliating death imaginable just to keep us from it. (Doesn't sound like anyone too interested in roasting people to me.)

You see, the problem is not with God; it's with us. We're the ones who told Him to get lost; we're the ones who told Him to take a hike back in the Garden of Eden. And even today when we sin as individuals we're saying exactly the same thing: "Leave me alone, God. I want to do it my way, not Yours."

Fortunately some of us eventually begin to realize our way is not so hot, and we want to come back to God. And for those who are serious, He has provided a way, an instantaneous way for us to get back into His presence: through the sacrifice Jesus Christ made for us on that cross.

The point is, we're the ones responsible for cutting God off; we're the ones responsible for this disease called sin. It's *our* fault, not His.

All this to say . . .

Hell is real. Very real.

And it's not too terribly hard to imagine. It is *complete and total separation* from God.

- Its *darkness* is the complete absence of *God's holiness.*
- Its *misery* is the complete absence of *God's love.*
- Its *torment* is the complete absence of *God's forgiveness.*

The Lord doesn't want anyone to experience that separation. In His intense love for us, God has provided the cure. And anyone, no matter who they are, no matter what they've done, can receive that cure and return to God's presence, no strings attached. All they have to do is ask.

But if they don't want to, if they keep refusing God and continue to insist on being separated from Him, He will let them have their way—for eternity.

The Media—Are We Really What We Eat?

inally, brothers, whatever is true, whatever is noble, whatever is right, whatever is pure, whatever is lovely, whatever is admirable—if anything is excellent or praiseworthy— think about such things (Philippians 4:8).

If you're looking for a bunch of rules and regulations on what to watch or listen to, forget it. By now we've all heard the horror stories about rock music, TV, and films, so I'm not going to waste your time with a bunch of do's and don'ts.

The decision is yours. You're the guardian of your mind, and what you choose to feed it is up to you.

But as a full-time writer and film director, I'd like to share a little more of what goes on behind the scenes to help you make those decisions.

It's Everywhere

First of all, we're all bombarded by the media. It has become a major factor in most of our lives. In fact, according to a Nielsen survey, "Today's typical high school student has logged at least 15,000 hours before the screen—more time than he has spent in any other activity except sleep."

Other surveys seem to indicate that we spend more time absorbing information from the media than we do from our teachers, friends, churches, or parents. And for this reason many sociologists count

77

the media as *one of the greatest single forces* shaping our lives today.

In fact, a study by J.L. Singer at Yale University states: "The outlook on *any* moral value can be changed through TV viewing." Think of that for a moment. Any moral value you have can be changed through the media. *Any moral value.* Now that's power.

And there's nothing wrong with that type of power, nothing wrong with helping to shape a person's outlook—if it's for the good. But who determines what is good? Not you. Not me. The people who make those decisions are the top executives in charge of the media corporations. Now many of them are good people with good motives. In fact, according to George Barna and William Paul McKay in their book *Vital Signs* (Crossway), "Two out of three TV executives suggested that television should promote social reform." And, "The select few who have control of the medium are consciously striving to transform American society, through television, to conform to their vision of what is right and desirable."

Like I said, those are great motives. But the problem lies in what *they* consider "right and desirable." Is it the same as what you and I would consider?

To get a better handle on their outlook, here's a survey of some of the top TV executives in the country:

- 7 percent of television executives regularly attend church.
- 97 percent are in favor of women having the right to abortion.
- 80 percent feel there is nothing wrong with homosexuality.
- 51 percent believe there is nothing wrong with adultery. (From Linda Lichter, S. Robert Lichter, Stanley Rothman, "Hollywood and America: The Odd Couple," *Public Opinion*, January 1983, pp. 54–58; and Lifestyle Trends in America, survey by

the American Resource Bureau, Wheaton, Illinois, as quoted in *Vital Signs*, pp. 56–57.)

I don't know about you, but I'm not crazy about people with that moral outlook getting inside my head and trying to "conform" *my* thinking to what *they* consider "right and desirable."

And since many executives look upon Christianity as something narrow-minded and repressive, it's doubtful you'll see much of Christ or His principles on the ol' tube.

I know of one Christian in the story department of a major TV series who is constantly putting in references to God and is constantly getting them removed. It's not because the executives are "evil," but because they simply disagree with the Christian concept of God and morality. Of course, my friend can expect the usual excuse, "We just don't want to offend our viewers." (This is always good for a laugh since no one's concerned about offending when it comes to murder, adultery, and language; but when it comes to mentioning God, everyone suddenly becomes very concerned about "offending.")

Anyway . . . let no one tell you there isn't prejudice in Hollywood. There is. I've experienced it, and so have most of my Christian friends. It's not always conscious, but it is always there. And if you're a Christian, much of it is directed against what you believe.

MANIPULATION

As a writer and director my primary objective is to manipulate you. I'm only successful if I can get you to cry, to laugh, to ache, and be thrilled exactly when I want you to. All the years I've trained, all the dialogue I write, every camera angle I choose, and all the music I use is designed for one reason and one reason only: to manipulate your emotions. If I succeed and really grab you, you'll tell all your friends, they'll tell theirs, and suddenly I have a hit. That's the name of the game. And few things feel as good to moviemakers as watching the audience cry when we want them to cry and laugh when we want them to laugh.

Now don't get me wrong; manipulation is not necessarily bad. I like getting caught up in a good story as much as the next guy. All I'm saying is when you step into the theater or turn on the tube, be aware that somebody out there is trying to manipulate you; then decide if that is the picture or show you want to be manipulated by. If it is, fine. If not, pass. Because you will not go away unaffected. Let me repeat that: *You will not go away unaffected.* We've gotten too good at doing what we do.

Unfortunately, not all professionals in the media use their skills just to entertain or present their view of the world.

Not long ago I knew of a well-known actor that a beer company kept asking to make a commercial. It was a great idea and destined to be a tremendous hit and a classic for years. The offer was very tempting, but because of his new faith in Christ the actor just didn't think he should make it. So the company kept offering him more and more money and the temptation kept growing until, unable to stand anymore, he finally went in to see the vice-president of the company.

"Why is it so important to you fellows that I make this commercial?" he asked.

The V.P. smiled. "That's easy. Our reports show that you have a strong following of kids from the ages of 9 to 13. We want them."

The actor walked out—he had his answer.

That's just one example. What about the more subtle manipulations that have convinced us to equate fat with failure, love with lust, success with things, holiness with narrow-mindedness?

Millions of dollars are spent every year to find out how best to get your attention, to make you feel what we want you to feel, and to make you buy what we want you to buy. In short, all that money is being invested to find out how to pull your strings.

The same goes for music. I talked with a guitarist who plays with a super famous rock star known for his crazy, anything-goes lifestyle. On stage this superstar will stagger over to the bottle of Jack Daniels and chug down a healthy swig to everyone's cheers and applause. What no one bothers to tell the audience is that it's all a show. A way to grab them and make them believe he's living a wild, reckless, carefree life . . . a life that they can also enjoy. No one bothers to tell them that they're being lied to and manipulated. No one bothers to tell them that it's Lipton tea inside that bottle.

Now What?

There are the facts. So what do we do with them? Smash the set, boycott the movies, burn the albums? (Even if I were to suggest this, I'm afraid the only thing that might get burned is this book.)

What you can and should do is be very cautious and very, very selective. It's true, the media's power can be used for good. That's why I and many others are in it. If you can find the good and edifying things, go for it. But if you can't, stay away. I mean, you've only got one mind. Why let someone get inside and mess it up?

I'm telling you the absolute truth. To this day there are scenes I would literally pay money to have removed from my memory. As it is, they'll stay with me the rest of my life; they will always haunt me, and there's nothing I can do about it.

Television

To be quite frank, if I were not in the business I'm in, I would probably have sold the TV set by now. Granted, there are some excellent shows on from time to time, but I often feel like I'm wading through a garbage dump for just a scrap of edible food.

Besides the constant danger of TV subtly chipping away at my values, there are some other drawbacks:

- *Hampers relations.* Who wants to sit around talking and relating with the family when they can get wrapped up in a fantastic, action-packed, no-commitment fantasy?
- *Destroys time.* Studies show that the average amount of time Americans watch TV is 3.3 hours per day (from American Resource Bureau, as quoted in *Vital Signs*, p. 51). That's nearly 24 hours every week and *52 days every year!* Imagine what we could do with that full extra day each week, those 52 extra days each year if we were to invest them in ourselves or in God? That's exactly how the great preacher David Wilkerson (founder of Teen Challenge and author of *The Cross and the Switchblade*) got started. He simply set aside all those hours he'd spent in front of the set and began using that time to pray. As a result his life (and our world) has never been the same.
- *Requires little intellect.* The general rule of thumb for TV writers is to write for someone at junior high level. "Don't challenge the audience," they say. "Don't make them think." In fact, sitcoms are often referred to in the business simply as "mind-candy."
- *Distorts reality.* Real life becomes a bore. I mean, what can compare to the fast-paced, special-effect, music-filled action-adventures? Or the hot 'n' steamy passions that are supposed to be real love? (It's amazing how many divorces are happening because couples think love is supposed to be like what they see on the screen.) Also, it can create unrealistic expectations of ourselves that may lead to depression and even self-hatred.

Now it's also true: TV can educate, it can entertain, and it has the potential for much good. All I'm suggesting is that you be careful. Make sure you're the one using it—don't let it use you.

Motion Pictures

Unless I need to see it for business purposes, I will not go to an R-rated film. (When my friends and colleagues razz me I just laugh it off and say I'm not old enough. They get the message.)

Again, be smart. Ask around. Check out the posters, the ads. Do they contain scenes that you don't want roaming around inside your mind? Do they touch on a certain weakness you know the Lord is working on? (Violence and profanity have never been problems for me. And if necessary I might see an "R" if that's why it has that rating. But since sensuality has always been a battle inside my head, I won't even go near a "PG" if I know it has sexy situations.)

Again, just be smart. You've only got one mind. Don't let anyone dirty it up.

Music

Ah, yes, the great battlefield. "To listen or not to listen, that is the question." There are probably as many opinions on this as there are people to give them. But the bottom line is that a lot of music (Christian and non) is great, and a lot is garbage. And as with TV and film, you cannot make any hard, fast rules. It's up to you to use your own God-given discernment.

Although there are no "carved-in-stone" rules, here are a few guidelines that you may want to consider in choosing what to buy or listen to:

Are the lyrics and music uplifting? Do they help you see life more clearly, enjoy it more deeply, understand how God would have you live it more fully? In other words, do they *give* to your life instead of trying to *steal* from it? (Remember to look past the superficial—a lot of times Satan appears to be giving when he's really stealing.)

Do they help you appreciate some aspect of our Creator or His creation? Do they stir up the joy, the peace, and the love He has surrounded you with? Or do they try to steal these gifts—replacing them with resentment, desire, unrest?

The bottom line: Does the music in one way or another draw you closer to the Lord or help you enjoy His abundant life? Or does it drag you into the world and its dead-end mentality?

All this to say . . .

Whether we like it or not the media has a powerful effect on our lives—on what we think, what we feel, what we believe. And whether we like it or not the old adage is true: We really are what we eat.

If we fill our minds with garbage, rest assured that's what we'll become. But if we do a little work to find out what's good and digest that, then that's what we can become.

Once again the decision is ours. . . .

> Finally, brothers, whatever is true, whatever is noble, whatever is right, whatever is pure, whatever is lovely, whatever is admirable—if anything is excellent or praiseworthy—think about such things (Philippians 4:8).

CHAPTER 9

Death and Suicide

Death is a reality.

No matter how much we hate it or try to ignore it, it's still going to happen—to each of us. Count on it. As the playwright George Bernard Shaw put it, "The statistics on death are quite impressive. One out of one people die."

WHY?

Dying is definitely not on my top–10 list of things to do. It separates, it destroys, it deprives. There is nothing harsher than ripping someone away from friends and loved ones, destroying all hopes and dreams, and depriving them of all that they could do and all that they could be.

So why? Why, if there's a loving God, did He invent such a miserable thing? Why does He make us go through it?

Unfortunately, just like suffering, death wasn't in God's original game plan. Death wasn't God's choice; it was ours.

> When Adam sinned, sin entered the entire human race. His sin spread death throughout all the world, so everything began to grow old and die, for all sinned (Romans 5:12, TLB).

So death comes as a direct result of sin. But before we come down too hard on Adam, remember the Bible says we're all guilty, "for *all* sinned."

But for those of us who realize we've made a mistake—for those of us who want to start following God's plan—as always, He's provided a way out.

Adam's *one* sin brought the penalty of death to

many, while Christ freely takes away *many* sins and gives glorious life instead. The sin of this one man, Adam, caused *death to be king over all*, but all who will take God's gift of forgiveness and acquittal are *kings of life* because of this one man, Jesus Christ (Romans 5:16–17, TLB).

That doesn't mean we can skip death like some class we're ditching. But for the Christian, instead of a time of fear and agony, death becomes more like graduation day: a time for moving onward to bigger and better things.

So what's it like? We've touched on this when we talked about heaven and hell. Here's a little more of what you can expect if you have turned your life over to Christ.

Immediately With Jesus

Contrary to what some teach we are not doomed to

- floating around and haunting houses
- making guest appearances at seances
- coming back in different lives until we finally get it right
- falling into a deep sleep until Jesus returns
- going to some holding pen (purgatory) until our sins are paid off.

Instead, as best as we can understand from the Scriptures, as soon as we die we go to be with Jesus. Billy Graham, in his book *Facing Death and the Life After*, explains it like this:

The believer's passage to heaven is a direct route. As soon as we are dead, we will be with the Lord. Jesus told the repentant thief on the cross, "I tell you the truth, today you will be with me in paradise" (Luke 23:43). Paul de-

clared, "I desire to depart and be with Christ"
(Philippians 1:23). He also affirmed, "There-
fore we are always confident and know that as
long as we are at home in the body we are
away from the Lord. We live by faith, not by
sight. We are confident, I say, and would pre-
fer to be away from the body and at home with
the Lord" (2 Corinthians 5:6–8) (p. 238).

Will We Recognize One Another?

Lots of people who have clinically died and then
come back to life talk about meeting friends and loved
ones who have already died and who come out to greet
them as part of some welcoming committee. But again,
keep in mind these are only personal experiences; they
are not from Scripture.

There is, however, some scriptural indication that
we'll recognize one another. Back in Luke 9 a couple
heavyweight Old Testament heroes who hadn't been
around for centuries dropped by for a little chat.

Seems Jesus was on a mountaintop with some of His
disciples when suddenly Moses and Elijah appeared
and started talking with Him about His upcoming
death on the cross. It's doubtful these guys were wear-
ing any name tags, but somehow, some way, the disciples immediately recognized who they were.

OK, so as soon as our physical body dies, our spirit
goes to be with the Lord, and we'll probably all recognize one another. But it doesn't stop there. Eventually,
when Jesus returns to earth, we'll go through another
transformation. When Jesus returns from heaven to set
up rule on earth, our old, decayed carcasses will be resurrected from the dead and changed into brand new
bodies.

SUPERHUMAN BODIES

When he comes back he will take these dying
bodies of ours and change them into glorious

bodies like his own (Philippians 3:21, TLB).

A body "like His own." Not a bad deal, considering that with His resurrected body Jesus was in perfect health and was able to do things like walk through closed doors, suddenly appear to people, zip up to heaven. And we're not talking some sort of ghost or spirit here. He did all of these things with a physical body that could actually eat and that people could actually touch.

So if you think you got the short end of the stick with a crummy body now, rest assured it won't always be that way.

> Yes, they are weak, dying bodies now, but when we live again they will be full of strength. They are just human bodies at death, but when they come back to life they will be superhuman bodies (1 Corinthians 15:43–44, TLB).

What Do We Do Up There?

No offense, but if all we do in heaven is sit around playing harps and floating on clouds, that doesn't sound like my idea of paradise.

Mine either.

The good news is the Bible never talks about harp plucking or cloud floating. What it does talk about is being able to really get into loving and praising and worshiping God and becoming like Jesus.

Oh, there's one more thing we'll be doing: helping Him rule the universe.

Find that a little hard to swallow? I did. At first it sounds a little farfetched. But it's right there in the Book:

> To him who overcomes, I will give the right to sit with me on my throne, just as I overcame

and sat down with my Father on his throne (Revelation 3:21).

The Spirit himself testifies with our spirit that we are God's children. Now if we are children, then we are heirs—heirs of God and co-heirs with Christ, if indeed we share in his sufferings in order that we may also share in his glory (Romans 8:16–17).

And finally:

Do you not know that the saints [that's us] will judge the world? . . . Do you not know that we will judge angels? (1 Corinthians 6:2, 3).

Pretty impressive. To really worship Jesus, *and* to share in His glory, *and* to help Him rule the universe— well, that sounds like a program worth signing up for.

SO WHAT?

But what's all this got to do with me now, today?

A good question. And the answer is simple: "Everything." Because how we live today is going to determine how we live after we die. Let me say that again. What we do now is going to have a direct effect on how we spend eternity.

First, there's the heaven-or-hell decision. Do we want to take the punishment for our sins and suffer in hell, or do we want Jesus to take that punishment so we can live in heaven? A stupid question, I know. Unfortunately, too many people are coming up with an even more stupid answer.

But what about those of us who've made the right decision and are heading to heaven? Does how we live now really make any difference on how we live then? Heaven is heaven, right?

Yes and no. We'll all be there, true—*but* each of us

will be *judged* and *rewarded* by how we served God down here.

> For we will all stand before God's judgment seat. . . . Each of us will give an account of himself to God (Romans 14:10, 12).

> So we make it our goal to please him, whether we are at home in the body or away from it. For we must all appear before the judgment seat of Christ, that each one may receive what is due him for the things done while in the body, whether good or bad (2 Corinthians 5:9–10).

You see, if we've asked Jesus to take the rap for our wrongdoings and to become our Lord but we spend all our time down here pursuing selfish pleasures and goals or building our lives with things that don't really count . . . well, according to the Bible, we may be in for a little disappointment:

> No one can ever lay any other real foundation than that one we already have—Jesus Christ. But there are various kinds of materials that can be used to build on that foundation. Some use gold and silver and jewels; and some build with sticks, and hay, or even straw! There is going to come a time of testing at Christ's Judgment Day to see what kind of material each builder has used. Everyone's work will be put through the fire so that all can see whether or not it keeps its value, and what was really accomplished. Then every workman who has built on the foundation with the right materials, and whose work still stands, will get his pay. But if the house he has built burns up, he will have a great loss. He himself will be saved, but like a man escaping through a wall of flames (1 Corinthians 3:11–15, TLB).

In other words, if you build your life with eternal

things (love and service to God and fellow folks), you'll have phenomenal rewards in heaven. If you build your life with worthless stuff (money, fame, and selfish desires), you'll make it to heaven OK if you're a Christian, but you won't have anything to show for your life but ashes.

Suicide

There is nothing more tragic than the act of someone taking and destroying his or her own life, especially when that person is young with an entire future ahead.

And yet suicide is the number two killer of teens in America. This year alone, two *million* teenagers will attempt suicide. *TWO MILLION!* That's nearly 5,500 young people a day!

Why? What's going on? And more important, what can we do to help?

LIFE IN THE PRESSURE COOKER

There is no other time of life where you'll be going through so many changes and have to make so many decisions as during your teen years. In those few short years from age 13 to 19 you're suddenly thrust out of cozy childhood and forced to make major choices about

- who you are
- what you believe
- how you'll live your life
- what you'll do with your life
- what your standards are.

And if that's not enough there's

- school
- peer pressure
- sexual pressure
- social pressure
- parent pressure

91

- loneliness
- self-acceptance
- radical chemical changes
- first loves
- no loves
- that ever-transforming body.

ROLLER-COASTER EMOTIONS

There is no other time in your life that you will experience such exhilarating highs—and such devastating lows. You're in the midst of a thousand first-time experiences, and first-time experiences are always the best—and the worst. It's a roller-coaster ride full of Death Valleys and Mount Everests. As you get older, these peaks and valleys start to level out because you have other experiences to compare them with. But for now they can be tough.

When older adults hit long-term bad situations, they know from experience that they won't last forever. But when young people enter deep, long-term heartache or depression, they can grow terribly hopeless—they have no past experience to prove to them that things will eventually get better. So they take the ultimate escape.

But what's so sad is that if they'd have waited, or if they would have gotten help, the pain and hopelessness would have eventually disappeared. Emotional wounds are just like physical wounds. It may take time, it may take outside help, but if you're willing to take that time and get that help, they will *always* heal. *ALWAYS.*

WHAT CAN I DO?

If you're reading this now and think life isn't worth the hassle, that there's too much pressure or that you're in a pit too deep for anyone to help, please, *please* talk to somebody. There are people who have been where you are, people who have seen nothing but utter blackness and hopelessness. And yet, by talking to someone, they've managed to make it through those troubled waters.

You see, Jesus wasn't fooling when he called Satan a "thief' who wants to "steal and kill and destroy." Don't let the little creep have his way. Get help. Find somebody you can trust, somebody you can talk freely to, somebody who knows how to listen. Maybe a pastor, a youth worker, a counselor at school, or just a *mature* friend in Christ.

You do not need to fight this battle on your own. Christ loved you enough to die for you. Give Him a chance to help. He made you special and unique, and He has a lifetime of hopes and plans for you. Please don't short-circuit Him; please don't cut Him off before He really gets you started.

Just as He said Satan came to kill and destroy, He promised that He (Jesus) came so "that they [you] might have life, and might have it abundantly" (John 10:10, NASB).

You may not see it yet, but that's His plan. Just give Him a chance to get it in full operation.

If You Know Someone

If someone you know is talking about suicide, be his or her friend. Don't try to preach or to be some sort of cheerleader. Just listen and ache and cry with your friend. That's part of what Jesus did with His suffering friends, and that's some of the best help any of us can offer.

If the situation arises, tactfully offer words of hope. Try to help your friend see the bigger picture—that the pain will go away and that God's got a lifetime of better things in store. And above all, let someone you both trust, like a counselor or pastor, know as soon as possible.

Can't Suicide Make Situations Better?

That's usually what the person who attempts it thinks. But here's what John Q. Baucom, in his book *Fatal Choice, the Teenage Suicide Crisis*, says:

> Even at their best, suicide attempts are devastating to the family and the victim. Successful suicides are even more damaging. The emotional trauma experienced by family and friends ranges from extreme guilt to denial, rage, and profound anguish. People blame themselves for not noticing. Eventually they even blame each other as the reality becomes more confusing. It is quite common for families of both unsuccessful and successful suicide attempts to eventually experience depression themselves and occasionally additional attempts.
>
> Many people who attempt suicide do so under the misconception that it will "make things better." In my professional experience *I am aware of no cases where that has been true* (Moody Press, p. 95, italics added).

Will Someone Who's Committed Suicide Go to Hell?

No one can say for sure, but I doubt it. Not if he or she has really made Jesus Lord. The whole reason Jesus came was to forgive us of our sins, no matter how terrible they may be. And suicide, no matter how rebellious toward God's plans or how selfish and self-centered, is not a sin that God is unable to forgive. I personally believe He can and will forgive anyone who has seriously accepted Jesus and has asked Him to forgive his sins.

> For I am convinced that neither death nor life, neither angels nor demons, neither the pres-

ent nor the future, nor any powers, neither height nor depth, nor anything else in all creation, will be able to separate us from the love of God that is in Christ Jesus our Lord (Romans 8:38).

All this to say. . .

Death is a horrible, destructive thing that we human-types have brought upon ourselves through sin. But, as always, God has taken something horrific and, for those who follow Him, has turned it around into a type of blessing—a graduation into a life full of His presence.

> Death has been swallowed up in victory. Where, O death, is your victory? Where, O death, is your sting? . . . Thanks be to God! He gives us the victory through our Lord Jesus Christ (1 Corinthians 15:54–55, 57).

CHAPTER 10

How Can I Raise Happy Parents?

Bringing up your folks through those teen years can be pretty frustrating. . . .

One minute they seem like normal freedom-loving Americans, and the next they're pulling dictator tactics, destroying anything that vaguely resembles liberty. One minute you're able to judge precisely what they'll do, and the next they suddenly turn irrational and seem to be doing their best imitation of Larry, Curly, and Moe.

And what about their timing? Why are they never there when you want them, and always underfoot, trying to "relate," when you don't?

The answer lies in one word . . .

TRANSITION

Theirs and yours.

You're leaving childhood and making the transition into adulthood. Every week you're slightly different from who you were the week before. And it's not always consistent—one day you may feel like taking on the world, and the next you may just want to crawl into Mama's lap and have a good cry. And to top it off, you're now walking around in an adult body with an adult intellect, but still having to deal with semi-adult emotions. It's enough to make a person schizoid. And, in fact, you are . . . a little. But that's only normal and natural. It comes with this rapidly changing time of your life; it comes with *transition*.

So it's little wonder your folks are neurotic—I mean, they're never quite sure who they're going to be dealing with. The first 11 years you were a piece of cake; changes came but they came slowly and somewhat predictably. But now . . . "Let's see, it's Tuesday; I wonder who Julie's going to be today?"

Not only are your parents dealing with your transitions, but they've got their own set of changes to worry about. What are they going to do when you're out of the nest? How will they relate to each other? And what about getting old? Their days of changing the world, of reaching all their goals, are quickly coming to an end. And just around the corner lurks the possibility of (gulp) . . . grandparenthood.

All this to say that these few years may be a little turbulent. Relationships with your parents (or caretakers) may get a little bumpy. But if you know what to expect and follow these four common-sense principles, there's no reason why you all can't enjoy the ride.

1. Understanding

The key to coexisting with anybody is to try to understand where they're coming from, to try to "walk a mile in their shoes." Parents with teens are going through almost as many pressures as their kids are, and the best way to get along with them is to understand them.

So first of all, keep in mind that regardless of your age your parents will always, *always* feel . . .

RESPONSIBLE

They will feel responsible for who you are, what you do, what you become. You are literally a part of them. Your failures become their failures; your successes, their successes. And whether you believe it or not, when the final line is drawn, most parents would count your life more important than theirs; most would lay down their lives to save "their baby's." No wonder they're always on your case. Most of the time they've done their best not to shortchange you, and now they just want to make sure you don't shortchange yourself.

Keep that in mind the next time they chew you out for bad grades, or for "wasting" time, or because of who you hang out with. Try to keep that in mind when they go into verbal overkill with the five-point lecture. Their timing, their approach, their frustration, their anger may be all wrong. But the bottom line somewhere beneath it all is that they're still trying to look out for *your* best.

Another tough responsibility they have is knowing just how much freedom to give you and when. Unfortunately there are no set rules, no handbooks to see how late you can stay out, when you can use their car, where you can go and with whom. It all depends on what they feel you can handle. Too much freedom and they can destroy you. Too little freedom and you can explode with frustration.

For what it's worth, few teenagers ever feel they get enough freedom—and most parents fear they've given too much! But as the teen proves more and more responsible with the freedoms that are handed out, that final umbilical cord between parents and child will be cut—not overnight, but during those six years from 12 to 18.

There will be mistakes . . . on both sides. Count on it. But be patient. Try to understand the difficulty parents have in making their decisions. And if you don't like their final decision, pray that God will change their minds. Don't bet on it, but it has been known to happen.

OUTSIDE PRESSURE

Besides feeling all that responsibility for you, your folks have a lot of outside pressure to deal with. The president of your dad's company chews out your dad's boss. The boss lays in to your dad. Your dad explodes at your mom. Your mom explodes at you over some minor thing and threatens to ground you for life!

True, this isn't exactly fair. And when things cool down it wouldn't hurt to bring it up. But until then don't take it personally. Sometimes the world can be a pressure cooker, and instead of channeling their anger and frustration in the proper direction, parents will occasionally dump it on those they're closest to. Again, it doesn't make it right, but understanding that your folks are out there getting clobbered by the world may help you understand where they're coming from.

REJECTION

No matter how well parents may pretend to handle the fact that their baby is growing up, they will always feel some rejection. As you enter adulthood you're no longer trusting in every word they say; you're no longer going to them for all the advice, or information, or counsel . . . or even love.

This can be pretty traumatic for them when you stop to think about it. I mean, at one time they were all you lived for, they were the number one all-time hit of your life. And now with your hectic schedule, new friends, and new romances, they may wonder if they're even on the charts. Help them out. Try to make this transition as easy as possible for them. Try to include them from time to time. Let them know they still count.

GUILT

I don't know of a single parent of a teenager who isn't struggling to one extent or another with guilt. Every time a son or daughter slips up or gets hurt, there's something in the back of the parent's mind that says, *You see, if you would have just taken more time with her, if you had just been a better parent, this never would have happened.*

Most of you already know what a sensitive area this is. Pushing the guilt button can work wonders in manipulating parents. Want something? Just remind them how one of their million failures deprived you in the past and, bingo, instant gratification.

Ah, guilt, the gift that keeps on giving.

Resist the temptation to lay a guilt trip on them. Go easy. In fact, if possible, you might even let them know it's OK to be human, that you respect them even when they do make mistakes.

So that's step number one. Try to *understand* where your parents are coming from. Realize that they don't wake up in the morning and say, "Oh boy, it's Thursday—this is the day I get to ruin Ramona's day."

Like everyone else, parents usually try to be rational human beings. It's just that circumstances sometimes make that nearly impossible.

Now on to step number two. . . .

2. Forgiveness

This is somewhat related to the first step, but not exactly. You don't have to figure out why a person behaves the way he does in order to forgive him. Jesus did not say, "Forgive people only if you can understand why they're doing what they're doing." He said flat out, "Forgive. Period. End of discussion."

When parents are unreasonable, when you're accused of something you're totally innocent of, when a brother or sister is obviously getting a better break, when you're telling the absolute truth and no one believes you . . . don't hold it in *and don't hold a grudge*.

If you're being shafted, wait until tempers cool, and in a day or week or month (maybe even after you've served your sentence and have nothing to gain), bring up the subject again. Let them know that they really were wrong, that it hurt you, *and that you've forgiven them*. Don't just let it pass. It must be dealt with. And you'll be surprised at what that sort of *gentle* honesty will do for you, for your relationship, and in affecting their future decisions about you.

Finally, a word has to be said about parents who can't control their impulses, parents who abuse their children physically, sexually, or emotionally. If this is happening to you, get some help—immediately. It *does not* mean the parent doesn't love you; it just means your mom or dad has a problem—and it's a problem that neither of you can handle on your own. It *must* be handled by professionals, like your pastor or a counselor at school. It's not your fault and you are not to blame. The important thing is to stop it.

It will not go away by itself. Help is needed. It may be embarrassing and at first your parent may not even admit to it. But the point is, if you really love your parents, then *get that help.* They deserve it and so do you. As impossible as it seems, people are being healed of these problems all the time and families are constantly being brought back together and made whole. It is possible. All it takes is courage (to get that help), along with plenty of love and forgiveness.

3. Honor

When we're little tykes we're absolutely positive that our parents can do no wrong. I mean, they're practically the fourth part of the Trinity. But as we grow we start to see that they actually do make mistakes. Their *humanness* starts to show more and more and our contempt starts to rise. This, coupled with the fact that we're starting to evaluate and solve situations more independently, may cause us to wonder if they'll *ever* be right again. Fortunately (for both sides) this only lasts a few years, and eventually we realize that just because their way of solving a problem is *different* doesn't necessarily make it *wrong*. Mark Twain said *something* like: "When I was 15 I was appalled at how stupid my father was. But by the time I turned 21 I was amazed at how much the old man had learned in six years!"

God has a lot of thoughts about how we should respond to our parents, and He doesn't pull any punches:

> Anyone who curses his father or mother must be put to death (Exodus 21:17).

In fact, of all Ten Commandments, only one of them promises us something for obeying:

> Honor your father and your mother, so that you may live long (Exodus 20:12).

It doesn't take a nuclear scientist to figure out there's more to honoring than just obeying. We've all been in positions where we go ahead and do something they say, but every step, every movement, every thought is screaming our real attitude of "Contempt, contempt, contempt!"

If you're having a hard time honoring your parents, ask the Lord for help. (He doesn't give us a command without supplying the power to follow it.) Look for opportunities to show that honor. If necessary, force yourself to show it. Try to realize that even though you may disagree with them, they've still got a few decades of experience on you and maybe, just maybe, there is some hidden (perhaps *very* hidden) wisdom to go along with it.

Oh, one last note on honoring. Scripture says, "A man reaps what he sows" (Galatians 6:7). It's amazing, but as you start to show honor to your parents, they'll eventually start to show honor toward you. . . . "Gee, Milfred's really been respecting my decisions lately. He's really showing some signs of maturity. Let's go ahead and give him the car for the evening."

"Golly, Harold, that's a great idea. In fact, why don't we buy him that Jaguar he's been dreaming of?"

"What a keen idea, Mable! Let's do it now!"

Well, that may not be how it always works, but I think you get the idea. Honoring becomes a cycle. The more you give, the more you eventually receive. So if you want honor and respect from your parents, start priming the pump. Eventually it'll come back to you "pressed down, shaken together and running over" (Luke 6:38).

4. Communication

As we've said before, communication is the key to any relationship. Whether it's with God, someone we're romantically interested in, or even our parents, the best way to work things out is to talk. And the best way to talk is to be around from time to time to do it.

I know it's tough when the whole world is out there begging you to come along and join in. But try to leave some time just for you and your family. Not only is it good for relationships, but it's good practice for when you have your own family and have to learn to shut out the world for time with them.

When you do talk, watch your attitude; try to do it in honor. Avoid accusing or inflammatory statements. Nothing puts people more on the defensive (and less likely to respond positively) than blaming them for something. Instead of, "You're such a dictator! You never trust me with anything!" how 'bout, "I understand your point, but maybe together we could come up with a solution better for both of us." You may not find a Jaguar parked in the driveway, but by taking the time to be quiet and rational, and not forcing somebody to be defensive, your conversations will always be more productive.

Practice "active listening." People love to talk, to voice *their* feelings. But the best communicators are the ones who listen and ask questions. Find out what's really on their minds; help them get what's really bothering them off their chest. And once the air is clear you'll be able to have a real conversation with much better results.

Finally, be willing to be wrong. At this stage in life when it's so important to prove you're responsible, to prove that you can be right—turn the tables on them. Admit that you might be wrong. Ask for advice. Although it may go against every fiber in your body, admitting mistakes and asking for advice is one of the surest signs of maturity.

All this to say. . .

These transitional years from childhood to adulthood can be tricky. But they don't have to turn into a setting for World War III. If you make a decent effort in these four areas—*understanding, forgiving, honoring,* and *communicating*—there's no reason why you all can't come out survivors . . . and maybe even enjoy the process.

CHAPTER 11

What About All This Occult Stuff?

The occult seems to be growing by leaps and bounds these days. Everywhere you look you see people fooling around with astrology, Ouija boards, fortune-telling, se-ances, Satanism, or buying into the latest hype on Eastern spiritualism, UFOs, or reincarnation. In fact, I've written an entire book series called FOR-BIDDEN DOORS that explores these various issues.

But why are they so tantalizing and popular?

Because every person has a built-in spiritual hunger. And whether they know it or not, con-sciously or unconsciously, they're looking for some-thing to fill it—be it through drugs, the occult, or other conscious-altering practices.

And if they don't turn to God to fill that hun-ger, that spiritual void, there's somebody else out there willing to do it.

Unfortunately, that somebody else has motives 180 degrees different from the Lord's.

God wants to fill that void because He loves us and wants to make us "mature and complete, not lacking anything" (James 1:4). Satan wants to move in so he can take over, turn us into slaves, and even-tually destroy us.

BIG difference.

It's little wonder then that God, for our own good, has a few choice tidbits to say on getting in-volved with the occult:

> Do not allow a sorceress to live (Exodus 22:18).

Do not turn to mediums or seek out spiritists, for you will be defiled by them. I am the LORD your God (Leviticus 19:31).

A man or woman who is a medium or spiritist among you must be put to death. You are to stone them (Leviticus 20:27).

Demons

Demons are very real. As far as we can tell they are probably those angels that were cast out of heaven with Satan (2 Peter 2:4; Revelation 12:9). And unfortunately they are usually what people fool around with when they get into the occult. Those are not departed spirits that people deal with in seances, or with Ouija boards, or in haunted houses. Those are not UFO creatures communicating through telepathy and channeling. Those are not reincarnated lives being recalled through hypnosis. In the legitimate situations (where there is no fakery or subconscious involvement) those voices, impressions, automatic writings, or whatever come from your basic, run-of-the-mill demons. Here are a few more of their characteristics found in the Bible (compiled by Josh McDowell and Don Stewart):

- Demons are spirits without bodies (Ephesians 6:12).
- Demons are numerous (Mark 5:8–9).
- Demons have supernatural powers (Revelation 16:14).
- Demons can sometimes inflict sickness (Matthew 9:32–33).
- Demons can possess or control animals (Mark 5:13).
- Demons can possess or control humans (Luke 8:2).
- Demons know that Jesus Christ is God (Mark 1:23–24).
- Demons teach false doctrines (1 Timothy 4:1) (*Un-*

derstanding the Occult, Here's Life, pp. 47–49).

And according to Scripture, it's often the demons themselves that we are battling with when we fight various difficulties in life:

> For our struggle is not against flesh and blood, but against the rulers, against the authorities, against the powers of this dark world and against the spiritual forces of evil in the heavenly realms (Ephesians 6:12).

But before we give these creeps too much credit, keep in mind that the best news about demons is that if we are Christians, they have to obey US:

> I have given you authority to trample on snakes and scorpions and to overcome all the power of the enemy; nothing will harm you. However, do not rejoice that the spirits submit to you, but rejoice that your names are written in heaven (Luke 10:19–20).

Now, that doesn't mean we go out demon-hunting or looking for them behind every bad time or unexplained event. But it also doesn't mean we totally ignore that they're around. As usual the answer lies somewhere in between.

One of the main problems of today is that in people's search for spirituality, many are leaving themselves wide open to deception or even possession by these demons. I know beyond a shadow of a doubt that many become possessed when they purposefully give up control of their minds or bodies through transcendental meditation, seances, mind-altering drugs, some forms of hypnotism, and other practices of the occult.

Nothing's for free. And if people want a supernatural experience through these means, rest assured there're a whole lot of beings out there willing to make sure they get it . . . as long as they can have *"controlling* interest."

Ouija Boards

Ouija boards have been around a long time, some experts believe since as far back as 600 B.C. But their purpose has always been the same: to communicate with the so-called spirits of the dead.

And what does God have to say?

> Let no one be found among you who . . . practices divination or sorcery, interprets omens, engages in witchcraft, or casts spells, or who is a medium or spiritist or *who consults the dead.* Anyone who does these things is detestable to the LORD (Deuteronomy 18:10–12, italics added).

Today's version of the Ouija board is a flat, smooth board with letters and numbers on it. A pointer mysteriously moves under the hand of the "player" and spells out the answers to whatever question is asked. What makes today's board so dangerous is that it's treated as a toy. In fact, it's sold as a party game in department and toy stores around the world.

It's true, this and a lot of occult practices can be faked or subconsciously manipulated by the "player." But, unfortunately, that's not always the case. Edmond Gruss, an occult expert, makes this statement about the Ouija board: "The content of the message often goes beyond that which can be reasonably explained as something from the conscious or subconscious mind of the operator." He continues:

> The board has been subjected to tests which support supernatural intervention. The testing of the board was presented in an article by Sir William Barrett, in the September 1914 *Proceedings of the American Society for Psychical Research* (pp. 381–394). The Barrett report indicated that the board worked efficiently with the operators blindfolded, the board's alpha-

bet rearranged and its surface hidden from the sight of those working it. It worked with such speed and accuracy under these tests that Barrett concluded: Reviewing the results as a whole I am convinced of their supernormal character, and that we have here an exhibition of some intelligent, disincarnate agency mingling with the personality of one or more of the sitters and guiding their muscular movements (p. 394, as quoted in *Understanding the Occult*, p. 96).

And since Satan never gives anything for free, people who experiment with the board often have a costly price to pay. Again, quoting from Edmond Gruss:

The many cases of "possession" after a period of Ouija board use also support the claim that supernatural contact is made through the board. Psychics and parapsychologists have received letters from hundreds of people who have experienced "possession" (an invasion of their personalities). Rev. Donald Page, a well-known clairvoyant and exorcist of the Christian Spiritualist Church, is reported as saying that most of his "possession" cases "are people who have used the Ouija board," and that "this is one of the easiest and quickest ways to become possessed" (Edmond Gruss, *Cults and the Occult in the Age of Aquarius*, as quoted in *Understanding the Occult*, p. 96).

UFOs

It may seem odd to include UFOs under the occult since so many of them have either been faked or can be explained through natural phenomena. In fact, 95% of reported sightings have a normal, logical explanation. But for those 5% that can't be explained, here are some interesting facts from my book *The Encounter* from the

"FORBIDDEN DOORS" series:

> Most reputable researchers believe the appearances are real, but not physical. If they are physical they would have to follow physical laws.
>
> They don't. For instance . . .
>
> Most sightings have been reported to travel between 1,000 and 18,000 miles an hour. Yet no person has ever reported hearing a sonic boom.
>
> The objects are often seen coming to instant stops. What happens when you are inside a car traveling at 20 or 30 miles an hour and it suddenly stops? Imagine the same effect if you were traveling several thousand times faster.
>
> Many UFOs are seen streaking across the sky, then making abrupt right-angle turns. The force of making a right-angle turn while traveling at only 5,000 miles an hour is strong enough to sheer in half a solid steel ball, let alone destroy any living creature inside.
>
> Most researchers believe that *if* UFOs exist they don't come from other worlds but other dimensions, i.e. the spiritual world.
>
> With that in mind, consider the following facts:
>
> 1. Most "alien" messages are autowritten or spoken through humans in exactly the same method that occultists use to channel demons.
>
> 2. Their messages frequently emphasize the NON-deity of Jesus Christ.
>
> 3. They generally insist man will never be judged by God.
>
> 4. Many of these channelers experience the exact physical and mental symptoms of people who are possessed by demons: nausea,

hallucination, antisocial behavior, and hearing voices.

5. Reports of so-called alien abductions are increasing. However, it is interesting that nearly every abducted person studied has had previous involvement with the occult (from *The Encounter* [Tyndale House], with additional information supplied by Dr. Hugh Ross, *ETs and UFOs*, Pasadena, CA: *Reason to Believe* 1990 audio cassette).

Astrology

I also hesitate to put astrology under the occult heading. But since there's no chapter on jokes and rip-offs, I'm afraid this will have to do. It's interesting that even God mocks those who take astrology seriously:

> Let your astrologers come forward, those star-gazers who make predictions month by month, let them save you from what is coming upon you. Surely they are like stubble; the fire will burn them up (Isaiah 47:13–14).

Astrology is the belief that our lives are controlled by the position of the stars in the sky. The theory is interesting but has a few holes:

- It was conceived and based on the idea that the stars rotated around earth. (Most of us by now have discovered that's not true.)
- There are several different versions of astrology with many in direct opposition to each other. For instance, some believe there are 8 signs of the zodiac, others believe 12, 14, or even 24.
- It's pretty hard to find any two astrologers who will give the same advice to the same person on the same day.
- And what about twins? Here are two people born

113

with the stars in the same position, and yet the events of their lives are never identical.

Even with these holes and a total lack of any scientific evidence, God is still down on practicing it. Why?

- It takes away our freedom of choice. People who believe in it feel they are no longer responsible for their decisions. After all, they say, "It was in the stars—what else could I do?"
- It's fortune-telling, turning to sources other than God for our hope, our future, and our well-being.
- It's a form of manipulation. Since we're all prone to suggestions, if somebody or something tells us we will be doing a certain thing, we may just find ourselves starting to do it.

STAY AWAY

All this to say . . .

There're a lot of occult practices going on these days, but that shouldn't be too much of a surprise. After all, we've been warned that it would happen:

> The Spirit clearly says that in later times some will abandon the faith and follow deceiving spirits and things taught by demons (1 Timothy 4:1).

Be smart. Just because it can be proven that some supernatural event happened, that doesn't necessarily mean God is behind it. Lots of other critters out there are trying to get your attention . . . and more. God didn't give us all those warnings for *His* health; He gave them for *ours*. Be smart. Stay away.

But if you should find yourself in the middle of a confrontation with demons, there's no need to be afraid. You have the authority. You have the Creator of the universe on your side. All you have to do is use that authority *in Christ's name* and the little creeps have to obey. It may not happen in the first five seconds; they may test, they may taunt, they may try to frighten. But if you hold fast to Christ, the authority is *always* yours:

> I have given you authority to trample on snakes and scorpions and to overcome *all* the power of the enemy; *nothing* will harm you (Luke 10:19, italics added).

CHAPTER 12

How Come We're So Right?

ow come, of all the religions in the world, ours just happens to be the right one?

A good question, and one we shouldn't be afraid to ask. After all, God doesn't need a bunch of mindless Christians stumbling around in the dark who can't answer the simplest question about their faith.

"So, tell me, Johnny—why do you believe?"

"Because."

"I see. And why's that?"

"Because I believe."

"And the reason you believe?"

"Because I do."

The good news is you don't have to commit mental suicide to be a Christian. God created our whole being—body, spirit, and *mind*. And He wants to minister to all three.

It's true that as we mature in Christ, the Lord seems to spend less and less time with our logic and more and more time with our faith. And that only stands to reason. Once we've made the decision that He can be trusted and we've given our lives to Him, there's no reason for God to keep proving himself over and over again.

But at the start it's a good idea to lay down a firm foundation of facts and truth. To know why we believe what we believe. Once that foundation is laid and we've decided to fully trust Christ, our faith will be able to stand strong—to endure whatever the enemy throws at it.

So . . .

Can We Really Trust the Bible?

Since so much of our faith is based on the Bible, it's probably a good idea to see if it's really true. After all, it's a pretty old book with some pretty weird tales. How do we know they weren't just made up? Or that they haven't been changed over so many centuries? You know, a dash more miracles here, a pinch more of the supernatural there. . . . How do we really know?

Well, first of all Scripture itself claims to be inspired by God: "All Scripture is inspired by God" (2 Timothy 3:16, NASB).

Not some Scripture, not most Scripture, but "*all* Scripture.*"

And by "inspired" we don't mean that someone got so worked up about God that he got all inspired to invent a bunch of stories for Him. When translated from the Greek, the word "inspired" actually means "God-breathed."

Think of that for a moment. The very breath of God Almighty, His very life is somehow incorporated in every page, every sentence, every word of Scripture.

But there are more reasons for believing Scripture is true other than just because it says so.

Over and over again, Jesus Christ quoted from Scripture. He knew it backward and forward. He treated it as if it was absolute, 100 percent fact. And if it's good enough for Him, it should do for us.

ARCHEOLOGISTS AND HISTORIANS

For decades historians and archeologists have been uncovering historical writings and ancient artifacts that prove the Bible is accurate. There are more than a few books written about the various archeological and historical findings and how they confirm Scripture. But Millar Burrows, a Yale archeologist, put it best when he said:

> Archeological work has unquestionably strengthened confidence in the reliability of the Scriptural record. More than one archeologist has found his respect for the Bible increased by the experience of excavation in Palestine (Millar Burrows, *What Mean These Stones?* [Meridian Books], as quoted in *Evidence That Demands a Verdict* by Josh McDowell, Here's Life, p. 66).

BUT IT'S SO OLD. . . .

Well, maybe the Bible was originally inspired by God, but it's been copied and handed down for so many centuries. How do we know that the version we're reading is the version He inspired?

Good question.

First of all, since the pages (they were actually scrolls back then) eventually wore out, special men were hired to make *exact* copies of the originals. And you'd better believe they took their job seriously. In fact, here are just a few of the rules those poor fellows had to follow every time they sat down to work. . . .

- They had to wash their entire body.
- They had to sit in full Jewish dress.
- Each line had to contain exactly 30 letters.
- Each letter had to be separated by the width of a hair.
- They could not write a word, not a single letter from memory.
- The very ink itself had to be prepared with a specific recipe! (according to *Hebrew Text of the Old Testament* by Samuel Davidson, as quoted in *Evidence That Demands a Verdict*, pp. 56–57).

These and many more rules and regulations make it

119

pretty clear that they knew exactly what they were dealing with. No one was about to make a mistake, and you'd better believe that no way was anyone going to try to slip in a little "creative editing" on God.

THE DEAD SEA SCROLLS

The discovery of the Dead Sea Scrolls gives us another reason to believe that the Bible we have today is the same as the one God originally inspired. In 1947, a shepherd boy stumbled on a cave with several hidden jars that contained scrolls of Scriptures (including the entire Book of Isaiah). And when the scientists investigated those scrolls, they found some to date from as far back as 120 B.C.!

At last it was time for the great showdown. If your Bible was the same as those Scriptures that were over 2,000 years old, it would prove that it had remained virtually unchanged from the time God first inspired it. But if those Scriptures were different from our current Bible, it would prove that people had tampered with God's Word over the centuries and that it could no longer be trusted. Carefully the experts went over the text—back and forth, checking every phrase, every word, every letter. They knew the gravity of their findings.

And the result?

According to Gleason Archer in his *Survey of the Old Testament* (as quoted in *Evidence That Demands a Verdict*), the Isaiah copies "proved to be word for word identical with our standard Hebrew Bible in more than 95 percent of the text. The 5 percent of variation consisted of obvious slips of the pen and variations of spelling."

The test had been passed. In over 2,000 years, the Word of God had remained virtually unchanged!

Who Is Jesus?

Since Christianity is basically centered on one person, let's spend the rest of the chapter examining that person. Is Jesus Christ really who all the Christians say He is? Is He really God the Son?

First of all, it's important to keep in mind that the Bible isn't the only historical book that mentions the existence of Jesus. There were other Jewish and Gentile historians in those first couple of centuries who wrote about this miracle-worker from Galilee. The most famous is probably a Pharisee by the name of Josephus. He wrote:

> Now there was about this time Jesus, a wise man, if it be lawful to call him a man, for he was a doer of wonderful works, a teacher of such men as receive the truth with pleasure. He drew over to him both many of the Jews, and many of the Gentiles. He was the Christ, and when Pilate, at the suggestion of the principal men among us, had condemned him to the cross, those that loved him at the first did not forsake him; for he appeared to them alive again on the third day; as the divine prophets had foretold these and ten thousand other wonderful things concerning him. And the tribe of Christians so named from him are not extinct at this day (as quoted in *Evidence That Demands a Verdict*, p. 82).

OK, so we know Jesus really existed. But how can we be sure he's really the Christ—"the Anointed One," the only Son of the Father?

PROPHECIES

From the time Adam and Eve first sinned, God began promising to send somebody who would tromp on Satan for them and provide a way back to God (Genesis 3:15). As a result, the Old Testament is filled with hundreds of prophecies about what this Redeemer, this Savior of the world, would be like.

All are from the Old Testament and written several

hundred years before Jesus ever came on the scene—yet they point clearly to one man and one man only . . . Jesus Christ.

Here are just a few of those Old Testament prophecies and where they were fulfilled in the New Testament by Jesus.

HIS BIRTH

> Therefore the Lord himself will give you a sign: The virgin will be with child and will give birth to a son, and will call him Immanuel [God with us] (Isaiah 7:14), *Fulfilled in Luke 1:26–35 and Matthew 1:18–25.*

HIS MINISTRY

> But later on He shall make it glorious, by the way of the sea, on the other side of Jordan, Galilee of the Gentiles. The people who walk in darkness will see a great light; those who live in a dark land, the light will shine on them (Isaiah 9:1–2, NASB), *Fulfilled in Matthew 4:12–16.*

> Then will the eyes of the blind be opened and the ears of the deaf unstopped. Then will the lame leap like a deer, and the tongue of the dumb shout for joy (Isaiah 35:5–6), *Fulfilled throughout His ministry.*

HIS TRIUMPHAL ENTRY INTO JERUSALEM

> Rejoice greatly, O Daughter of Zion! Shout, Daughter of Jerusalem! See, your king comes to you, righteous and having salvation, gentle and riding on a donkey, on a colt, the foal of a donkey (Zechariah 9:9), *Fulfilled in Matthew 21:1–11.*

HIS CRUCIFIXION

And since Jesus' dying on the cross for our sins is the pivotal point of Christianity, it only stands to reason that there would be lots of prophecy regarding it. Here are just a couple. Again keep in mind that they were written hundreds and hundreds of years before Jesus was ever born. . . .

> But he was pierced for our transgressions, he was crushed for our iniquities; the punishment that brought us peace was upon him, and by his wounds we are healed. We all, like sheep, have gone astray, each of us has turned to his own way; and the LORD has laid on him the iniquity of us all (Isaiah 53:5–6).

> A band of evil men has encircled me, they have pierced my hands and my feet. I can count all my bones; people stare and gloat over me. They divide my garments among them and cast lots for my clothing (Psalm 22:16–18).

And the list goes on and on, including the details that He would be given gall and vinegar to drink (Psalm 69:21), that He would be killed in between two thieves (Isaiah 53:12), that none of His bones would be broken (Psalm 34:20), and that he would be buried in a rich man's tomb (Isaiah 53:9).

Depending on your perspective, there are over 300 prophecies in the Old Testament that were directly fulfilled by Jesus Christ; *300!*

True, some of them could be called coincidences. But even if we were only to take 48 of the major prophecies, the chances of one man fulfilling all 48 would be incredibly high. In fact, the odds are 1 out of 10,000, 000, 000, 000, 000, 000, 000, 000, 000, 000, 000, 000, 000, 000, 000, 000, 000, 000, 000, 000, 000, 000, 000, 000, 000, 000, 000, 000, 000, 000, 000, 000, 000, 000, 000, 000, 000, 000, 000, 000, 000, 000, 000, 000, 000, 000, 000, 000, 000, 000, 000,

000,000,000,000,000,000,000!

Let's cut it back even further. Let's say Jesus didn't fulfill 300 prophecies, or even 48. Let's say He only fulfilled 8 of the major prophecies. The chances of one man fulfilling only 8 of the major Old Testament prophecies is 1 in 10^{17} . . . or the same odds as covering the entire state of Texas two feet deep in silver dollars, painting one of those silver dollars red, stirring them up, and telling a blind man he had one chance and one chance only to pick out the red one!

But Jesus didn't fulfill 8 prophecies, or 48. He fulfilled 300! (according to Paul Stoner, as quoted in *Evidence That Demands a Verdict*, p. 175).

HIS RESURRECTION

And then there is the matter of the Resurrection. The tombs of all other religious leaders in history are still filled with their remains. Only one is empty. Only one person was able to conquer death. I don't know about you, but if I had to choose a religious leader, I'd go for the one who has power and authority over the grave.

In fact, this is such strong proof that Jesus is God and such a clear "seal of approval" that people have been trying for 2,000 years to prove in one way or another that the resurrection of Jesus Christ was a hoax. But the Resurrection was so well-documented and verified that no one has *ever* been able to make a case against it stick. In fact, more than one author and historian who has tried to disprove it has actually wound up becoming a Christian!

Jesus' Claims About Himself

"OK, OK, I believe. And it's probably true, those prophecies probably were all about Him. I mean, everyone knows Jesus was a great teacher—just like Buddha,

Confucius, and Mohammed, right?"

It's a nice idea and one that lots of people use. The only problem is, it's *totally wrong*. You see, no "good teacher" would make the claims that Jesus made about himself. I mean, this guy claimed over and over again to be the greatest thing that would ever hit the world. Not only did He claim to be God's *only* Son, but again and again He claimed to be *equal* to God.

No good teacher would say that about himself—a raging egotist, maybe, or a loony-tunes crazy, but not a good teacher.

C.S. Lewis probably put it best when he said, "Either this man was, and is, the Son of God: or else a madman or something worse" (*Mere Christianity* [Macmillan], p. 56).

And in case you don't buy that, here are just a few of the claims Jesus made about himself:

> If you knew me, you would know my Father also (John 8:19).

> You are from below; I am from above. You are of this world; I am not of this world. I told you that you would die in your sins; if you do not believe that I am the one I claim to be, you will indeed die in your sins (John 8:23–24).

> I am the resurrection and the life. He who believes in me will live, even though he dies; and whoever lives and believes in me will never die (John 11:25–26).

> I am the way and the truth and the life. No one comes to the Father except through me (John 14:6).

> Anyone who has seen me has seen the Father (John 14:9).

> Father, the time has come. Glorify your Son, that your Son may glorify you. For you

granted him authority over all people that he might give eternal life. . . . Now this is eternal life: that they may know you, the only true God, and Jesus Christ, whom you have sent. I have brought you glory on earth by completing the work you gave me to do. And now, Father, glorify me in your presence with the glory I had with you before the world began (John 17:1–5).

All authority in heaven and on earth has been given to me (Matthew 28:18).

Did I say a few? Sorry about that. But there is one more Scripture I'd like to mention. It's my favorite and it's in John 8. We pick up where the Pharisees are outraged at Jesus' claim that if they keep His words they won't die. Now, as you read it, keep in mind that Abraham was their all-time great hero, a man who lived 2,000 years before Jesus ever came on the scene. We'll start where the Pharisees are really laying into Jesus:

"Now we know that you are demon-possessed! Abraham died and so did the prophets, yet you say that if a man keeps your word, he will never taste death. Are you greater than our father Abraham? He died, and so did the prophets. Who do you think you are?"

And Jesus' response?

"Your father Abraham rejoiced at the thought of seeing my day; he saw it and was glad."
"You are not yet fifty years old," the Jews said to him, "and you have seen Abraham!"
"I tell you the truth," Jesus answered, "before Abraham was born, I am!" (John 8:52–58).

Talk about gutsy. Talk about making a claim. And what's even more outrageous is that Jesus wasn't only claiming to exist before Abraham. There's a good chance He was using the exact name God used for himself back in Exodus when Moses asked God what He should be called.

God's response to Moses was simple: " 'I am who I am. This is what you are to say to the Israelites: "I AM has sent me to you" ' " (Exodus 3:14).

So not only did Jesus tell the Pharisees that He was around before Abraham, but if He was speaking Hebrew He was actually calling himself by the holiest name the Jews had for God, the very name God had called himself back when He was speaking to Moses. Jesus was calling himself the great "I AM."

No wonder the Pharisees tried to stone Him to death (John 8:59). Jesus was claiming to be God!

All this to say, we probably have to agree with C.S. Lewis (*Mere Christianity*, p. 56):

> You can shut Him up for a fool, you can spit at Him and kill Him as a demon; or you can fall at His feet and call Him Lord and God. But let us not come with any patronizing nonsense about His being a great human teacher. He has not left that open to us. He did not intend to.

What's All This New Age Stuff?

he last thing in the world I want to do is stand on some street corner and start screaming that something's from the devil. Talk about closed-minded. But I don't know what else to say about this subject. It seems to be everywhere and millions of people (including naive Christians) are being sucked into it every year. So . . . *"LOOK OUT, IT'S FROM THE DEVIL!"* There, thanks for letting me get it off my chest. Now let's see what "it" is.

A Nonreligion Religion

Although the New Age movement involves religious thinking, it is not an official religion with official headquarters, official spokespersons, or official leaders. It's more of a way of thinking than a religion. There are no fancy fireworks, fanfares, or telethons. Instead, the New Age movement spreads like water; it keeps a low profile while managing to seep, almost unnoticed, into our society—from the Star Wars film sagas to Saturday morning cartoon magic and mysticism to some relaxation techniques used in schools—the list goes on.

On the surface most New Age thinking sounds really great. Often the goal seems to be to get us more in tune with God and to help us become all that He designed us to be. What could be better or more spiritual? In addition, New Age thinking often uses Christian phrases, biblical concepts, and even parts of the Bible. And most of the New Agers will readily admit that Jesus Christ is God's son.

So what's the problem?

The problem is that it's a con job. Not the people, mind you. They're usually good, sincere folk. But they've bought into a false bill of goods. It's true they are drawing closer to a supernatural force all right—the only problem is, it's the *wrong* one.

Once you get past all the positive thinking, fancy phrases, and Christian-sounding concepts, you eventually discover something much darker. You discover that New Age thinking can be boiled down to one thing: it is simply a hodgepodge of demonic practices from the Eastern religions with just enough Christianity thrown in so we'll swallow the bait. Unfortunately it isn't until the bait goes down that people discover there's a hook buried inside.

SOME TIP-OFFS

Usually New Age thinking will involve some sort of belief or practice in

- reincarnation
- astrology
- mystical and out-of-body experiences
- channeling (spirits speaking through a person)
- crystal power
- yoga
- meditation
- imaginary guides
- some forms of positive thinking
- certain relaxation techniques
- altered states of consciousness
- self-improvement programs.
- UFOs

Is It Really So Wrong?

Come on, not all of that stuff is so bad. A Christian can believe in some of it.

Let's take a closer look at a few of the major beliefs and practices, then compare them to what the Bible says.

REINCARNATION

I've just returned from a heartbreaking trip to Asia, where I saw incredible indifference toward human suffering. Children and adults were begging, dying, starving, rotting away with leprosy in the streets—and no one seemed to care. And the countries where the lack of concern was the worst were the countries who believed in reincarnation the most.

Why?

Reincarnation basically states that the life you live today is a direct result of the way you lived a past life. If you were a good guy in the past life, things are going to go better for you this time around. If you were a jerk the last time, you'll pay for it by coming back as a bottom-of-the-heap person.

So if I believe that today's suffering people are just paying for their past sins, why should I interfere with "God's punishment" by trying to make their lives easier? In fact, it would be better for me *not* to help the poor and suffering so they'll hurry up and die and graduate to a higher lifestyle the next time around.

Now picture an entire society living under that type of thinking for centuries and you can start to understand why they have such intense poverty and disrespect for human life.

And yet, with such clear-cut examples of what reincarnation thinking does to society, today one out of three American college students believes in it. *One out of three.* And sadly, many of them say they are Christians—even though belief in reincarnation is in *direct opposition to the Bible*.

Reincarnation teaches that we keep dying and coming back to life. The Bible says,

> Man is destined to die *once*, and after that to face judgment (Hebrews 9:27, italics added).

Reincarnation goes against the very basis of Christianity. It teaches that the only way we can get rid of our sin is to go through several different lifetimes until we finally work it out. Jesus, on the other hand, says that He came to pay the entire price of our sins. In fact, that was the whole purpose of His dying on the cross—to pay for our sins. If we believed in reincarnation, we'd believe that we can eventually work our way into heaven and don't need Jesus Christ. Our salvation would lie in what we could do, not in what Christ has already done. The entire theme of the New Testament is that man can *never* be saved through his efforts—that he can *only* be saved by his faith in Jesus Christ (Ephesians 2:8–9).

Now there's one other minor problem. . . .

What about all these people who are supposedly taken back into their past lives through hypnosis? How do they know facts and foreign languages that they've never heard before if they did not live back then? Again, some of this can be fraud and some just an overactive subconscious. But for the legitimate experiences there can only be one answer.

Robert A. Morey puts it best: "A hypnotic trance is the exact mental state which *mediums* and *witches* have been self-inducing for centuries in order to open themselves up to spirit or demonic control. Hypnotic regression to a 'past life' can easily be an occult experience."

He continues with what I consider the biggest red flag about this practice:

Here lies the ultimate explanation for those "unexplainable" recall cases. In every situation where a person recalled a "past life," and this life was researched and proven factual in even intimate details, and not fraudulent, *the person was involved in occult practices.* Supernatural knowledge was gained by contact with satanic beings (*Reincarnation and Christianity* [Bethany House Publishers], pp. 24–25, italics added).

Those are not past lives they are recalling. They're not even past spirits. They are simply demons speaking through or starting to take over the thoughts of the person who had given up control of his or her mind.

CHANNELING

Channeling is nothing but your basic demon possession. Of course the latest twist is that these critters are supposedly UFO types or are people who have died. But it's all the same thing—people giving up control of their bodies for demonic spirits to come on in and take control. And what does the Bible say?

Let no one be found among you who . . . practices divination or sorcery, interprets omens, engages in witchcraft, or casts spells, or who is a medium or spiritist or who consults the dead. Anyone who does these things is detestable to the LORD (Deuteronomy 18:10–12).

Do not allow a sorceress to live (Exodus 22:18).

A man or woman who is a medium or spiritist among you must be put to death. You are to stone them (Leviticus 20:27).

But why? Is God afraid of a little competition? Hardly. It's simply that demonic spirits will always

God

New Age Thinking	Bible Truths
There are many ways that lead to God.	Jesus Christ is the *ONLY* way we can reach the Father. "I am the way and the truth and the life. No one comes to the Father except through me" (John 14:6).
God is not a specific person with a personality but a "force of the universe," *a la* Star Wars.	The Bible describes a specific God with a specific personality (Jesus taught us to pray, "Our Father which art in heaven," not "Some force which is everywhere"). God is a Father who loves, who aches, who gets angry, who forgives, and most important is someone who takes a personal interest in each of us (to the point of knowing how many hairs are on our heads).
God is both good and evil—"the good and dark side of the force."	"Your heavenly Father is perfect" (Matthew 5:48). In Habakkuk we read that His eyes "are too pure to look on evil" (1:13).

Jesus Christ

New Age Thinking	Bible Truths
Jesus Christ was the way to God in His time because He had "the Christ spirit" living in Him. But other people in other ages also had this same "Christ spirit," like Hercules, Krishna, and Buddha, and they were the way to God in *their* time.	A good clue of satanic influence is when anyone tries to raise up others to share in Jesus' glory. The Bible gives no room for such blasphemy. In fact Jesus himself clearly said, "*No one* comes to the Father except through me" (John 14:6, italics added), "I am the First and the Last" (Revelation 1:17), and "All who ever came before me were thieves and robbers" (John 10:8). The Bible states clearly that Jesus Christ is the one and only way to God in the past, present, and future.

Man

New Age Thinking	Bible Truths
Man is basically good.	Right. That's why we have so many wars and killings and injustices. The Bible clearly teaches that "all have sinned and fall short of the glory of God" (Romans 3:23), that we're born with this sin, and that the only way we can be free of it is through Jesus Christ.
Man is god.	This is exactly the same lie Satan used on Eve: "You will be like God" (Genesis 3:5). Hmmm.
Man can work his way into eternal paradise and Godlike perfection.	Once again they're saying there's no need for Christ's sacrifice on the cross, that we can do it on our own. Instead the Bible clearly states, "For it is by grace you have been saved, through faith—and this not from yourselves, it is the gift of God—not by works, so that no one can boast" (Ephesians 2:8–9).

take more than they give. And if you fool around and invite them in, there's a good chance they won't be leaving.

MEDITATION AND SPIRIT GUIDES

Another big fad these days is meditation—but not the type the Bible talks about. The Bible encourages us to "meditate" on God's Word and His greatness. New Agers tell us to let our minds go entirely blank. BIG DIFFERENCE. Because once we've created a vacuum inside, the New Agers encourage us to go to the second phase: inviting into that vacuum a "spirit guide" to "guide us into all spiritual knowledge and maturity."

Unfortunately it's been proven over and over again that no matter how beautiful and loving the spirit guide is (it may even claim to be Jesus), in reality it's your basic let's-possess-the-kid demon.

These are just a few of the basic New Age practices. Let's take a closer look at some of its basic beliefs.

New Age Beliefs

As we've seen, once you strip away the Christian-sounding phrases from New Age thinking, you wind up with a religion that is definitely hazardous to your health. But that's just the beginning. Because the New Age claims are also *directly opposed* to what the Bible teaches. The charts that follow give some prime examples.

THE KEY

The cross. The cross was the whole purpose of Jesus' life. The cross was the main reason He came down here. Yes, He said a lot of great things and yes, He cleared up lots of questions about who God is and what He's like— but over and over Jesus kept saying He came for one thing: the cross.

Again and again He said He came to take our punishment, to die on the cross so we could live.

> The Son of Man [Jesus] did not come to be served, but to serve, and to give his life as a ransom for many (Matthew 20:28).

There are other verses: Matthew 26:28; Luke 22:19–20; Luke 24:26; John 1:29; John 3:14–17; John 6:51; John 10:11; John 12:24–33; John 15:13, and the list goes on.

So no matter how Christian any teaching claims to be, it's a safe bet that *any belief or religion that says the Cross is not the very center of our relationship with God is NOT from God*. Can't get any simpler than that.

All this to say. . .

No one wants to start a witch hunt here or accuse every supernatural occurrence or everything we don't understand as being from the devil (God's also been known to pull off a few supernatural events from time to time). But be careful. Just because a person is experiencing the supernatural doesn't necessarily mean he's experiencing God. There are plenty of other supernatural creatures out there that would like to get your attention—and a lot more.

If you run across one of these new teachings or have a friend that is involved in one, check it out. Find out what it REALLY says about

- God
- Jesus Christ
- humankind

And most important, find out what it says about Jesus' sacrifice for us on the cross.

Wrapping Up

o there you have it, answers to some of the hottest questions by Christian teens. If you don't like the answers or if you have other questions, drop me a line or talk to your local youth worker or your pastor. You may even want to do the research on your own. God's really into people who like looking for truth. Just make sure you're looking in the right place . . . to the Source of all Truth. Because there is somebody else out there, "The Father of Lies," whose sole purpose is to deceive and kill and destroy.

But the good news is, if you're honestly seeking God, in whatever area, He'll be there to honestly answer your questions. Maybe not overnight, but when the time is right. Because He is the "rewarder of those who diligently seek Him."

You don't have to take my word on it.

In fact, you don't have to take anybody's.

Just grab His Book and check out what He has to say yourself. He's one person who will never, *never* give you a wrong answer.